Nikola Tesla

and the
Taming
of
Electricity

Nikola Tesla
and the
Taming
of
Electricity

Lisa J. Aldrich

MORGAN
REYNOLDS
PUBLISHING

Greensboro, North Carolina

NIKOLA TESLA AND THE TAMING OF ELECTRICITY

Copyright © 2005 by Lisa J. Aldrich

Library of Congress Cataloging-in-Publication Data

Aldrich, Lisa J., 1952-
      Nikola Tesla and the taming of electricity / Lisa J. Aldrich.— 1st ed.
            p. cm.
      Includes bibliographical references and index.
      ISBN 1-931798-46-X (lib. bdg.)
      1. Tesla, Nikola, 1856-1943—Juvenile literature. 2. Electric
engineers—United States—Biography—Juvenile literature. 3.
Inventors—United States—Biography—Juvenile literature. I. Title.
      TK140.T4A64 2005
      621.3'092—dc22

                        2004018786

Printed in the United States of America
First Edition

CONTENTS

ONE: CROATIA

Late on the night of July 9, 1856, lightning crackled ferociously as a midsummer storm passed over a farm near Smiljan, a small town in Croatia. Inside the farmhouse, Djouka Tesla was about to give birth to her fourth child. At the stroke of midnight, as the electrical storm still raged, a baby boy was born. His happy parents named him Nikola.

Milutin Tesla, Nikola's father, was the son of an army officer who had served under Napoleon. Milutin had tried to follow in his father's footsteps by joining the military, but he dropped out after an officer criticized him for not keeping his brass buttons polished. Milutin entered the ministry instead. He had a natural inclination for philosophy, wrote and published beautiful prose

Opposite: Nikola Tesla. *(Library of Congress)*

Nikola's father, Milutin Tesla. *(Tesla Museum Archives)*

and poetry, and preached eloquent sermons. He had an exceptionally good memory and could easily recite long passages of verse in several different languages.

Nikola's mother, Djouka Tesla, was the eldest daughter of eight children. She had been forced to assume maternal duties at a young age when her mother went blind. She was too busy caring for seven siblings to go to school to learn to read or write. Djouka's work ethic was strict and relentless. She arose before dawn and did not stop working until late at night. After her marriage she supervised the servants and ran the farm—growing all the crops, sewing the family's clothes, raising the children. She was artistically gifted; her needlework designs made her famous in the region. Djouka also loved to invent things. She made looms, butter churns, and kitchen tools, including a mechanical eggbeater.

Nikola—or Niko, as his family called him—his older

brother Dane (pronounced dah-nay), and their three sisters, Angelina, Milka, and Marica, spent an idyllic childhood in the countryside. Life on the farm was full of adventures. Nikola was an active boy who seemed to feel closer to animals than to people. He liked to try to ride the family cow and was often chased by the farm's ill-tempered gander.

Of all the animals on the farm, Nikola's favorite was Macak, the family cat. He later wrote of Macak as "the fountain of my enjoyment . . . I wish that I could give you an adequate idea of the depth of affection which existed between me and him." After dinner, Nikola and the cat would often run outside and play by Milutin's church, which was next door to the Tesla home. "We would just roll . . . and roll . . . in a delirium of delight. . . . Macak would grab me by the trousers. He tried hard

The house where Nikola was born in Smiljan, Yugoslavia, was destroyed during the Yugoslavian civil war in the 1990s, but this replica of the house, on the original house's exact site, was later built by the Croatian government.

to make me believe he would bite, but the instant his needle sharp incisors penetrated the clothing, the pressure ceased and their contact with my skin was as gentle and tender as that of a butterfly alighting on a petal."

While Nikola was at home with animals, he was not always as comfortable with people. One day when he was young, his two aunts came to visit. Tesla showed a trace of mischief when, as he later described the encounter, "They asked me who was the prettier of the two. After examining their faces intently, I answered thoughtfully, pointing to one of them, 'This here is not as ugly as the other.'"

Dane, seven years older than Nikola, was their parents' pride and joy. Like his mother, Dane was an inventor. He also liked to spend hours down at the shore of the nearby Adriatic Sea, listening to the fishermen's tales. He often brought the stories back to his family. Highly intelligent, the family expected him to accomplish great things. But when Dane was twelve, he was thrown off while riding the family's high-spirited Arabian horse. He died a few days later from his injuries.

It was a shattering tragedy for the Tesla family and it hung over Nikola the rest of his life. From then on, anything that Nikola accomplished caused his family to grieve because it reminded them of Dane's talents and the great things he might have been able to accomplish. Nikola grew to feel that his parents had rejected him, particularly his mother. He grew up having little self-confidence, for his accomplishments always paled in comparison to the memories his parents had of Dane's abilities.

Nikola shared his mother's love of invention and throughout his life attributed all of his inventive talents to her. Not all of his early inventions were successful. He once tried to use an umbrella as a parachute and jumped off the barn roof, expecting to glide gently to the ground. The resulting landing hurt him so badly that he was in bed for six weeks. When he recovered, he went back to swimming, fishing, and hunting frogs in the local creek with his friends. One of their favorite play-things was a waterwheel, which Nikola made when he was five years old. The other boys saw it as a toy, but the workings and potential of the wheel fascinated Nikola and inspired his later inventions.

He was also motivated by pride. Young Nikola and his friends planned a fishing trip to use some new fishing line and a hook they had been given. On the day of the trip, he had an argument with his friends and they excluded him from the adventure. They would not even allow him to see the new fishing line, but he did catch a glimpse of the hook as his friends ran away. He set about to make a hook of his own and go on his own fishing expedition. His hook did not have barbs and he did not use bait, but while the shiny hook was dangling above the water, a frog leapt at it and was snared. Much to the amazement of his friends, who caught no fish with their new hook and line, Nikola came home with two dozen frogs.

Though Nikola played with other boys his age, his hobbies and the way he seemed to always be deep in thought seemed strange to them. They did not always understand what he was up to. As a result, Nikola isolated himself from his peers as he spent more and more time on his inventions.

One of his most ingenious inventions was a propeller powered by insects. Nikola glued two very thin pieces of wood in the form of a cross, resembling the arms of a windmill. He glued the cross onto another piece of wood and attached a small pulley to the contraption. He collected a jar of June bugs and glued four bugs to each of the wooden blades. The bugs flapped their wings furiously in an attempt to escape, generating "power" and causing the propeller to turn at high speed. Recalling the incident in his later years, he wrote, "These creatures were remarkably efficient, for once they were started they had no sense to stop and continued whirling for hours and hours." Nikola's fascination turned to disgust when a neighbor boy came to visit. He spied some unused June bugs in a jar and proceeded to eat them alive. Nikola vomited, and, as he later recalled, "That disgusting sight terminated my endeavors in this promising field and I have never since been able to touch a June bug or any other insect for that matter."

Nikola was educated at the village school, where he quickly developed a passion for reading. His father had an extensive library, but Nikola was forbidden to touch any of the books. Nevertheless, he risked his father's anger by reading the books every chance he got. His love for reading was such that when his parents forbade him from reading after dark for fear that it would ruin his eyesight, Nikola stole candles to use in secret. Milutin found out and hid the candles. As Nikola later remembered, "I obtained tallow, made the wicking and cast the sticks into tin forms, and every night I would bush [plug] the keyhole and the cracks and read, often till dawn, when all others slept."

During this time, Nikola came upon a Serbian translation of *Abafi (Son of Aba)*, a historical novel by Miklos Josika, one of the first successful Hungarian novelists. The story awakened him to the possibilities of willpower and self-control, and Nikola began to discipline himself. He later wrote, "Had I a sweet cake or a juicy apple which I was dying to eat I would give it to another boy and go through the tortures of Tantalus, pained but satisfied. Had I some difficult task before me which was exhausting I would attack it again and again until it was done.

TANTALUS

In Greek mythology, Tantalus, the king of Sipylos, was the son of Zeus. His privileged ancestry made him a favorite of the gods, who granted him the honor of eating with them. But when Tantalus incurred their anger, their response was swift and severe. Most stories report that Tantalus insulted the gods by murdering his own son, Pelops, and trying to serve his body to the gods for dinner. When they realized what he had done, the gods brought Pelops back to life, then devised a fitting punishment for Tantalus. He was sunk into water up to his neck, but when he became thirsty and tried to drink, the water receded. A tree heavy with ripe fruit was just over his head, but when he became hungry and tried to eat, the wind would move the food away. Tantalus's punishment has come to symbolize something appetizing or appealing that is just out/ of reach—something tantalizing.

ARTHUR SCHOPENHAUER (1788-1860)

Nikola Tesla's early experiments with self-control reflect the teachings of the philosopher Arthur Schopenhauer. His most famous book, *The World as Will and Representation,* argued his belief that all of life was suffering and that desire caused pain. He went on to explain that the only possible relief from suffering would come by rejecting desire, a concept similar to that embraced by Buddhists. Schopenhauer was highly influential in the nineteenth century. His ideas influenced the writings of Russian Fyodor Dostoyevsky and the German philosopher Friedrich Nietzsche, among several others.

So I practiced day by day from morning till night. At first it called for a vigorous mental effort directed against disposition and desire, but as years went by the conflict lessened and finally my will and wish became identical. They are so today, and in this lies the secret of whatever success I have achieved."

When Nikola was seven his father was put in charge of a larger church in the nearby town of Gospic, where he was also assigned to teach religion at the local high school. This promotion meant the family had to leave the farm life that Nikola loved so much. He later wrote, "This change of residence was like a calamity to me. It almost broke my heart to part from our pigeons, chickens and sheep, and our magnificent flock of geese which used to rise to the clouds in the morning and return from the feeding grounds at sundown in battle formation, so perfect that it would have put a squadron of the best aviators of the present day to shame."

Living in the town of Gospic highlighted Nikola's social awkwardness. One Sunday after church, he finished ringing the bell in the belfry and came running down the stairs two or three at a time. A grand lady of Gospic, who always wore beautiful clothing and was accompanied by servants, was just crossing in front of the stairs on her way to shake Reverend Tesla's hand. That day she wore a floor-length dress with an enormous train brushing along the floor behind her. Nikola, in his exuberance, jumped from the third step to the bottom and landed squarely on the train, tearing it from her dress. The parishioners and his parents were horrified, and Nikola was so embarrassed that he avoided social situations for a long time thereafter.

He was redeemed on another Sunday, however, when the firemen of Gospic brought a new fire truck into town and lit a fire to demonstrate how well it worked. As the fire grew bigger, the firemen attempted to extinguish it with the hose, which was set up to draw water from the river. The hose, however, would not work, and the fire threatened to rage out of control. Young Nikola knew instinctively that there must be a kink in the hose under the water. He dove into the water in his Sunday clothes, disentangled the hose, and emerged from the river a hero. This act encouraged him to continue with his inventions, for he realized that his ingenuity brought him the love and approval of his parents and of society.

TWO: NEW HORIZONS

Between the ages of ten and fourteen, Nikola Tesla attended gymnasium, the equivalent of junior high school. The school was quite new and contained a well-equipped physics department. Nikola was fascinated by electricity from the beginning of his formal education. He read all that he could find on the subject and experimented with batteries and induction coils. Having devised a waterwheel as a boy, he now moved on to experimenting with water turbines. When he saw a photograph of Niagara Falls, he fantasized about putting a giant waterwheel under the falls and creating power from it.

During junior high school, Nikola came down with a serious illness. His doctors feared he might die. Because he was so sick, Nikola was allowed to read as many books from his father's library as he wished, including

TURBINE

A turbine is a machine that is used in the production of electricity. It converts the flow of air, water, steam, or gas into mechanical energy by powering the generator, which produces electricity. Waterwheels are primitive turbines, using the force generated by water to turn a wheel that then transmits its movement to machinery.

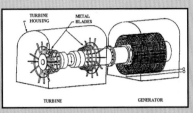

some that changed his life. As Nikola remembered, "One day I was handed a few volumes of new literature unlike anything I had ever read before and so captivating as to make me utterly forget my hopeless state." The books were the early works of Samuel Langhorne Clemens, a famous American author better known by his pen name, Mark Twain, who wrote humorous and satirical books, including *Tom Sawyer* and *The Adventures of Huckle-*

The gymnasium where Tesla attended school from age ten to fourteen. *(Tesla Museum Archives)*

berry Finn. Nikola began to recover soon after and became convinced that "to [Twain's books] might have been due the miraculous recovery which followed. Twenty-five years later, when I met Mr. Clemens and we formed a friendship between us, I told him of the experience and was amazed to

The author Mark Twain was an immensely popular figure around the world during much of Tesla's life. *(Library of Congress)*

see that great man of laughter burst into tears."

About this time, Nikola began having strange mental experiences that—initially—caused him great anxiety. Vivid images of places and objects would appear before his eyes, often accompanied by strong flashes of light. They were so real to him that he had a hard time distinguishing whether they were hallucinations or if they actually existed. He often implored his sisters to tell him whether the thing he saw before him actually was really there. It seemed as if he could reach out and touch the objects, but when he did his hand passed through them. He tried to banish the images by thinking of something else.

Nikola soon discovered that if he gave in to the

visions, they took him to wonderful places: "[A]nd so I began to travel—of course in my mind. Every night (and sometimes during the day), when alone, I would start on my journeys—see new places, cities and countries—live there, meet people and make friendships and acquaintances and, however unbelievable, it is a fact that they were just as dear to me as those in actual life and not a bit less intense in their manifestations."

In 1870, at the age of fourteen, Nikola moved from Gospic to Karlovac (now Carlstadt) to attend a four-year high school that offered more advanced courses than the

This map of the former Yugoslavia indicates several places of significance in Tesla's life.

Physicist Michael Faraday.

school in Gospic. He lived with his father's sister Stanka and her husband, who was a colonel in the army. At Karlovac, Nikola studied languages and mathematics, but his favorite course was physics.

The physics professor, Martin Sekulic, demonstrated many principles of physics, including electromagnetic induction, which made the generation of electricity possible. In 1831, the English physicist Michael Faraday had discovered that an electric circuit and a changing magnetic field would induce electricity to run through wiring. Tesla later wrote, "It is impossible for me to convey an adequate idea of the intensity of feeling I experienced in witnessing [Sekulic's] exhibitions of these mysterious phenomena. Every impression produced a thousand echoes in my mind. I wanted to know more of this wonderful force; I longed for experiment and investigation."

Suddenly Tesla began to see the usefulness of the

visions he had. He discovered that he needed no models or drawings of his inventions; he was able to visualize them as if they were actually in front of him. He did not need to build prototypes; in his mind he could construct his inventions, make them work, and even determine what changes or adjustments were necessary. Only when all the defects had been perfected in his mind's eye did he build the actual apparatus.

Tesla's mind worked so quickly, however, that many of his inventions were never built. After perfecting the invention in his mind, he became bored with it and his mind rushed to invent something new. Later in his life, his ability to work in his mind would hinder his work with other engineers, who demanded blueprints and diagrams. Tesla loathed drawing, and several times during his school years he was almost prevented from advancing to the next grade because of his problem with illustrating.

Despite this problem, Tesla managed to finish four years of high school in three. He had a gift for learning languages and mastered English, French, German, and Italian as well as several Slavic dialects. His forté, however, was mathematics. When a math problem was put on the blackboard, Tesla usually had the correct answer as soon as the teacher finished writing. At first the teachers suspected he was cheating, but they soon realized that his ability to calculate answers so quickly had to do with his abnormal ability to visualize and retain information.

Once Tesla finished high school, he faced challenges about his future. Since his birth, his parents had expected that he would someday join the clergy. The very thought filled Tesla with dread. He wanted to study engineering. His mood was made worse when his return to Gospic was marred by a horrible cholera epidemic. Corpses were stacked in the streets. Believing cholera to be spread through the air, instead of as it actually is by contaminated drinking water, the people of the town burned great piles of aromatic brush to cleanse the air of cholera germs. Tesla quickly contracted the illness, was bedridden for nine months, and nearly died. During one of the worst phases of the illness, Tesla told his father, "Perhaps I may get well if you will let me study engineering." His father replied that if he recovered, he would go to the best technical institution in the world. Tesla was soon better.

Nikola and his parents decided on the Polytechnic School at Graz, Austria, 175 miles to the north. However, the government had other ideas: facing a possible war with Turkey, the military expected all young men to complete three years of compulsory service. Tesla and his father were both pacifists. Milutin instructed his son to pack his gear and go into the woods. If Nikola kept a low profile and attracted no attention, maybe he could avoid being arrested and sent into the military. Meanwhile, he could fully recover his health, which was still fragile from his bout with cholera.

While in hiding, Tesla roamed the woods, thinking up

new inventions. He conceived of a "submarine tube . . . [able] to convey letters and packages across the seas . . . [and] a ring around the equator" for transporting people from one end of the globe to another. He also delighted in observing the way science worked in nature. One such discovery came when he was playing with snowballs on the side of a mountain. One snowball rolling down the mountainside "found just the right conditions; it rolled until it was a large ball and then spread out rolling up the snow at the sides as if it were a giant carpet, and then suddenly it turned into an avalanche . . . stripping the mountainside clear of snow, trees, soil and everything else it could carry with it." This surprising and awe-inspiring event revealed to Tesla that a small triggering event can unleash a great store of energy, the way that a single tiny spark can explode a ton of dynamite.

In 1875, after a year in the woods, Tesla returned to Gospic. The military still could have arrested him for fleeing its service, but his extended family included several high-ranking officers who most likely used their influence to obtain a deferment for him due to his poor health.

Tesla entered college at Graz on a partial scholarship and eagerly began his studies. At first, he planned to become a mathematics professor. He studied arithmetic, geometry, calculus, theoretical and experimental phys-ics, analytical chemistry, mineralogy, machinery con-struction, botany, wave theory, optics, French, and En-glish. He was especially pleased with his calculus instructor, Professor Allé, who he said "was the most brilliant lecturer to whom I ever listened. He took a special interest in my progress and would frequently remain for an hour or two in the lecture room, giving me problems to solve, in which I delighted."

Nikola studied more than twenty hours a day and soon changed his major to engineering. He also began to learn more languages—he fluently spoke nine in all—and studied the works of writers such as Descartes, Goethe, Spencer, and Shakespeare, learning long passages by heart. Tesla excelled in every class.

He returned to Gospic for the summer after his first year. Expecting to receive praise from his parents, he was surprised when his father instead tried to discourage him from returning to school the next semester. Tesla

A Gramme dynamo. (*Smithsonian Institute*)

did not know that some of his teachers had written letters to Milutin, telling him that they feared for Tesla's health due to his rigorous schedule.

Frustrated and angry, Tesla ignored his father's wishes and returned to school for a second year.

CURRENT
Current is the flow of electricity.

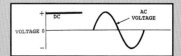

ALTERNATING CURRENT
Current is naturally alternating, meaning that it reverses direction at regular intervals. Imagine a river. Now imagine that the water suddenly changes direction and flows backwards, then forward again, then backward, and so on. The action of the river changing direction is called a cycle. Alternating current is electricity flowing along a wire that changes from going forward to backward to forward—one cycle. Alternating current is much more powerful and economical than direct current, as it can travel hundreds of miles without losing strength and needs no conduits.

DIRECT CURRENT
Direct current flows only in one direction. It is of limited use as its strength, or voltage, cannot be changed. Most batteries are DC, or direct current.

DYNAMO
An electric generator that produces direct current.

COMMUTATOR
A device used in electric motors and generators to change current from alternating current to direct current.

During Nikola's sophomore year in college, a Gramme dynamo, an electrical generator patented in 1870 by Belgian engineer Zénobe Gramme, was delivered to his physics class. As was customary, the dynamo was equipped with a commutator, a device that ensured the dynamo produced a direct current.

When the instructor, Professor Poeschl, demonstrated the dynamo, Tesla suspected that alternating current could be changed to direct current without using a commutator, but he did not know how to do it. Tesla bravely offered his opinion to the class, and the professor spent the remainder of the class period explaining why the idea of doing away with the commutator was preposterous. Poeschl even unhooked the commutator and declared with mock surprise that the dynamo no longer worked. This embarrassment galvanized Tesla. He would spend the next four years trying to prove his professor wrong.

Tesla began to encounter difficulties in his third year of college. He became bored and frustrated, having surpassed his fellow students in all subjects. They, in turn, ridiculed him for his study habits and resented him for being the professors' favorite student. Tesla began to gamble to console himself. He kept late hours playing cards, billiards, and chess. His father became very upset and could not excuse what he considered to be a senseless waste of time and money. Tesla told his father he could stop gambling whenever he pleased, but that he did not want to.

Once he became obsessed with finding an answer to the alternating-current dilemma, Tesla began gambling even more, sometimes staying up for twenty-four hours at a stretch. Whenever he won a great deal of money from one person, he always returned it to the loser, but when he lost money, his gambling buddies did not reciprocate his generosity. One semester he lost his entire allowance, including the money for his tuition. Tesla's father was livid, but his mother presented him with a roll of bills and said, "The sooner you lose all we possess, the better it will be. I know that you will get over it."

Tesla saw her words as a challenge. He won back his initial losses, returned the money to his family, and never gambled again.

As exam time approached, Tesla realized that he had squandered his study time with gambling and was completely unprepared. Though he was an excellent student, he asked the school for more time to study. When they refused, he did not graduate, nor did he receive grades for his last semester. Tesla's cousins had been sending him money but stopped when they found out he was no longer in school. Humiliated and ashamed, Tesla disappeared. His friends searched the countryside for him and finally decided he must have drowned in the river.

In actuality, Tesla had packed his belongings and traveled south into Slovenia. He arrived in Maribor in late spring of 1878 and began to look for work. He was soon hired by an engineer but did not stay at the job very long. He continued to travel south, ending up in Min-Gag, a small coastal village.

Tesla's parents were frantic with worry. His father finally located him in Min-Gag and urged him to return to the university. Tesla was adamant; he would not go back to Graz. Milutin offered another solution: he could change universities and make a fresh start. Tesla agreed and returned home with his father. He was accepted back into the family and began attending church once again

Tesla in 1879 at the age of twenty-three. *(Tesla Museum Archives)*

to hear his father's sermons. At church he met a young woman named Anna, whom he described as "tall and beautiful with extraordinary understandable eyes." Tesla was in love. The pair would take strolls by the river, sharing their dreams for the future. He wanted to be an electrical engineer; Anna wanted a family.

In 1879, Tesla's father died. Tesla was determined to fulfill his father's wish that he return to school, and in 1880, he traveled to Bohemia (now the Czech Republic)

TELEPHONE

Alexander Graham Bell (1847-1922) was born in Edinburgh, Scotland. Most of his inventions were made in his adopted home of Boston, Massachusetts. Because his mother was deaf, Bell had a special interest in the needs of deaf people. One of his inventions was a microphone to amplify voices. His work on the telephone was inspired by the telegraph—Bell hoped to be able to send voices through wire the same way Morse and others were sending signals. On March 10, 1876, he and his assistant, Thomas A. Watson, were preparing to test a new voice transmitter when Bell spilled some battery acid on his clothes. Watson was in another room when he was shocked to hear Bell's voice through the transmitter saying, "Mr. Watson, come here. I want you." Famously, Bell and a man named Elisha Gray applied for patents on the telephone the very same day— Bell beating Gray by just a few hours. The first telephone company, Bell Telephone Company, was founded on July 9, 1877. By 1884, long-distance connections had been made between Boston, Massachusetts, and New York City. The telephone grew in popularity as news of its invention quickly spread throughout the United States and Europe.

to enroll in the University of Prague. Though Tesla had hopes of continuing his relationship with Anna, she married another man a short while later.

Tesla's stint at the university only lasted the summer. Needing money, he left school to find work. His uncle Pajo suggested that he move to Hungary and work for the new telephone exchange, which an old military friend operated. Tesla moved to Budapest but found that the telephone company was not yet open. Desperate for a job, he sought work at the engineering department of the Central Telegraph Office of Hungary and was hired

The bustling city of Budapest, Hungary, in the late nineteenth century, where Tesla lived from 1880-1882. *(Library of Congress)*

as a draftsman and designer. Though the job paid very little, Tesla used whatever extra funds he had to buy equipment to conduct his own experiments.

Tesla ran into a former classmate at the Central Telegraph Office. Anthony Szigeti, who Tesla described as having "the body of Apollo . . . [and] a big head with a lump on the side . . . [that] gave him a startling appearance," became his best friend and confidant. Tesla enjoyed meeting Szigeti at local cafes, where the two friends talked, relaxed, and enjoyed challenging each other to good-natured games. One such game was a milk-drinking contest. Tesla lost one of these contests after drinking thirty-eight bottles of milk.

A few months after Tesla's arrival in Budapest, the telephone company opened and immediately hired Tesla and Szigeti. This was the first time that he came into contact with the work of Thomas Edison, a prolific American inventor who, in his lifetime, was awarded 1,093 patents. Though the phonograph (invented in 1877) and the incandescent light bulb (1879) are perhaps his most famous inventions, Edison also produced switches, sockets, electric motors, an electric pen, paraffin paper (used to wrap candies), and gummed paper tape (used to wrap packages). On September 4, 1882, Edison put into operation the first commercial power station, located on Pearl Street in lower Manhattan, providing electric light and power to customers in an area one-mile square.

Edison also made improvements on others' inventions. With his improvements on Alexander Graham Bell's telephone, he revolutionized communication. At the Central Telegraph Office in Budapest, it was Tesla's job to climb telephone poles to check lines and to repair equipment, and to serve on the ground as a mechanic and mathematician. He was also able to study commutators, generators, and dynamos that Edison had invented, some of which Tesla took apart and improved. Edison became his idol.

Though busy, Tesla's mind was never far from the alternating-current problem. He studied and restudied his own calculations, and pored over the work of others. He later explained his obsession: "With me it was a sacred vow, a question of life or death. I knew that I would perish if I failed." He gave up sleep, determined to prove that he was right and that Professor Poeschl and the rest of the world were wrong. His body and brain finally had enough, and he suffered a mental breakdown in 1881, at the age of twenty-five. He claimed that his pulse raced at 250 beats per minute, and that his body twitched and quivered uncontrollably. His senses became hyperacute: he could hear a watch ticking three rooms away. A fly landing on a table sounded like a dull thud. A horse and carriage passing on a street some distance away shook his body, and a train passing three miles away jarred him to the point of pain. He was unable to get any rest. His bed had to be put up on rubber cushions to enable him to sleep. The rays of the sun on his head caused him to wince in pain, and he claimed to have developed the sensitivity of a bat. He said he was able to detect the presence of an object by a peculiar creepy sensation on his forehead. A doctor examined him but gave up trying to diagnose his problem and simply told him that he was dying.

Tesla recovered, though, and he attributed his recovery to his strong will to live, his desire to continue his experiments, and to his friend Szigeti, who insisted that Tesla take long, healthful walks. It was on one such stroll in the park at sunset that Tesla found the answer to the alternating-current problem that so plagued him.

As Tesla watched the setting sun, large and orange as magnified by the atmosphere, he quoted from Goethe's *Faust:*

The glow retreats, done is the day of toil;
It yonder hastes, new fields of life exploring;
Ah, that no wing can lift me from the soil,
Upon its track to follow, follow soaring!

As soon as he finished reciting the poem, Tesla stopped as if he were paralyzed, not saying a word, his arms in midair. Szigeti feared that he was having a seizure and tried to get him to sit down on a park bench. But Tesla would not sit. The answer to his alternating-current problem had come to him in a flash. While gazing at the setting sun, Tesla had suddenly seen a whirling field of energy. He found a stick and drew a diagram in the soil. His diagram represented a new system that he called a rotating magnetic field in which two or more electric currents are not synchronous but are out of phase, or step, with each other. He could recreate a whirling field of energy by powering a motor whose magnetic coils were like the pistons in a car, some of which go up while the others go down. The resulting forces of magnetic attraction would cause the shaft of the motor to turn in a circle—the electrical equivalent of a wheel. All this would be accomplished with alternating current.

Tesla had eliminated the need for a commutator. He had proven Professor Poeschl wrong, and his rotating magnetic field would eventually revolutionize the technological world.

Tesla continued to experiment for several months. He later wrote of this time in his life, "In less than two months I evolved virtually all the types of motors and modifications of the system now identified with my name. . . . It was a mental state of happiness as complete as I have ever known in life. Ideas came in an uninter-rupted stream and the only difficulty I had was to hold them fast."

Ferenc Puskas, who had hired Tesla at the telephone exchange, now asked if he would be interested in moving to Paris to help his brother Tivadar Puskas run the new Edison lighting company there. In the three years since Edison had invented the light bulb, its use had quickly spread abroad from America. Tesla gladly accepted the job. Szigeti was also offered a job with the company, and in April 1882, the two friends set out for Paris on a new adventure.

THREE: EDISON

Tesla was overwhelmed by Paris. He wandered the streets of the city in awe. Never good at managing his money, he was usually unable to resist the temptation to buy any item that struck his fancy. Before long, he told his employer that, financially, "the last twenty-nine days of the month are the hardest."

Tesla led a strenuous life in Paris, arising early and, regardless of the weather, going from his apartment on the Boulevard St. Marcel to a local bathhouse on the Seine River, where he would swim twenty-seven laps. He then walked an hour to Irvy, where the Edison Lighting Company was located, and ate a large breakfast at 7:30 AM.

One of the workers at the telephone exchange was Charles Batchelor, a friend of Thomas Edison. Batchelor was an English engineer who had helped Edison to

This photomechanical print from the late 1880s shows Place du Châtelet and the Seine, not far from Tesla's left-bank apartment on the rue St. Marcel. *(Library of Congress)*

improve the telephone. They had supervised the installation of Edison's first commercial, self-contained lighting plant on the SS *Columbia*. Together they had watched the brilliantly lit ship sail down Delaware Bay on its way to California.

Impressed by Batchelor's experience, Tesla shared the idea for his rotating magnetic field motor with him in hopes that he would be interested enough to finance the building of the motor. Though impressed, Batchelor did not offer to back him financially.

Tesla's job required him to travel to various parts of France and Germany to repair equipment. He worked on the lighting of the opera house in Paris and the wiring

The Paris opera house where Tesla worked on the modernization of the lighting systems. *(Library of Congress)*

of a theater in Bavaria (a region of Germany). He was sent to Austria for a year to oversee the installation of generators.

Batchelor had urged Edison to test the generators before shipping them to Europe. Too many of them were causing fires. One such incident occurred in Strasbourg in 1883, when, at the opening ceremonies of a railroad station lighting plant, defective wiring caused a short circuit and a wall was blown out in the presence of the elderly Emperor William I. Austria refused to accept the plant, and the Edison Lighting Company suffered a serious financial loss. Because Tesla spoke both German and French fluently, he was appointed to travel to Strasbourg to try to straighten out matters and was promised a huge financial bonus if he succeeded.

Tesla accomplished his mission and returned to Paris in 1884, eagerly anticipating the promised bonus. But each of the three administrators to whom he appealed for the money denied having the authority to pay him. Tesla soon realized that they had no intention of paying him and resigned his position with the company.

Charles Batchelor urged Tesla to go to America, where, as he said, "the grass and the currency are greener." He wrote Tesla a letter of recommendation to give to Edison, and Tesla sailed for America in the spring of 1884 at the age of twenty-eight. When he arrived in New York after a miserable voyage, he had four cents in his pocket.

New York was a big shock to Tesla, as Paris had been earlier. Bustling and busily pushing forward with technological progress—the Brooklyn Bridge was being completed and the Statue of Liberty, a gift to the United States from France, was being hoisted into place—the huge city was rough, dirty, and unformed compared to older, more traditional Europe.

Tesla headed straight for Edison's lab. He asked the first policeman he saw for directions. On his way there, Tesla passed a shop and overheard the owner cursing a broken machine. Tesla stopped and offered to fix it. The shop owner was so grateful that he gave Tesla twenty dollars.

Thomas Edison was a very busy man—not just an

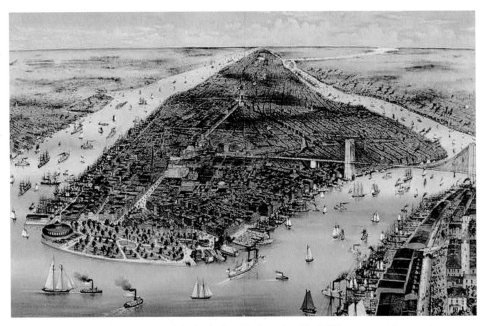

New York City, much as it looked when Tesla arrived in 1884. *(Library of Congress)*

inventor but also an entrepreneur and a shrewd busi-
nessman. He owned Edison Machine Works on Goerck
Street and the Edison Electric Light Company at 65 Fifth
Avenue. The generating station he owned at 255-57 Pearl
Street supplied lights to the entire Wall Street and East
River areas, including the mansions of a few hundred
wealthy New Yorkers as well as various plants, factories,
and theaters. He had a large research laboratory at
Menlo Park, New Jersey, that employed a number of
people. Edison was besieged by requests for electricity.
In particular, he received several requests to put self-
contained lighting plants on ships—a dangerous propo-
sition, in his opinion, because these plants often caused
fires. Electric lighting was still new, and some of the

products being used in its installation, including the insulation around the wires, were unsafe. A fire at sea usually ended tragically because sailors had nowhere to go to escape the flames.

Despite these safety issues, Edison's direct-current lighting of New York City had literally changed the landscape. Weblike masses of crisscrossed wires were strung from poles erected along the streets. Copper tubing was placed in conduits dug under the streets to carry the current to various destinations. Direct current cannot travel long distances, so Edison had to place a cumbersome and unsightly powerhouse every mile or so to generate more current. Few people really understood electricity at that time, and many were afraid of it— including the horses that pulled carriages down New York City's streets. Wary pedestrians carefully dodged

Edison's overhead electrical wiring not only presented dangers to pedestrians and horses, but also cluttered the cityscape. *(New York Historical Society)*

ELECTRIC TROLLEYS

Horse-drawn carriages were the preferred mode of transportation for centuries. But horses were expensive, messy, and had to be fed, watered, and stabled, cared for when sick, and disposed of and replaced when they died.

In the late 1800s, when the electric motor was perfected, people in charge of transportation in large cities saw a way to overcome the problems associated with horse-drawn carriages, and the electric street railway, also known as the trolley car or cable car, was invented.

Electric wires installed above the street powered the trolleys. Attached to each trolley car was a metal pole, on the end of which was a small wheel, or trolley, that touched the underside of the electric wires. The trolley car followed metal tracks in the streets. In 1887, the first electric street railway system was installed in Richmond, Virginia. Soon, the trolley became the favored means of transportation. Trolleys were much faster than horses so travel time was shortened, and the other problems associated with horses were eliminated. Trolley lines and rails soon extended beyond city limits, enabling people to live outside of the city center for the first time.

the tracks of electric trolleys, which often shocked the horses through their iron shoes and sent them bolting down the streets.

Tesla and Edison met on a particularly bad day for the American inventor. The Vanderbilt mansion caught fire after two electric wires had crossed behind a wall hanging, and a hysterical Mrs. Vanderbilt was demanding that the electrical installation be removed from her home, lest it cause another fire and burn down the entire house.

Edison sent a repair crew to the mansion, then turned

his attention to the next problem. The manager of the shipping company that owned the SS *Oregon*, was demanding to know when the dynamos for the lighting plant on the ship, which was losing money by the day while docked for repairs, would be fixed. Though Edison had no engineer available to send, he promised that one would be sent over that afternoon.

No sooner had Edison hung up the phone than a boy ran into his office and told him that a malfunctioning electrical junction box at Ann and Nassau Streets was leaking electricity and had catapulted a ragman and his horse into the air. Edison yelled for his foreman to get workers over there to fix it, if any could be found.

It was at this moment when Nikola Tesla entered the shop. Edison looked up to see a tall, dark-haired man with steel blue eyes standing in front of him. He asked impatiently what the visitor wanted. Tesla introduced himself and handed Edison the letter from Charles Batchelor. It contained one line: "I know two great men and you are one of them; the other is this young man." Edison scoffed audibly and asked Tesla what he could do.

Tesla began to describe the work he had done for Continental Edison in France and Germany. He then talked about his induction motor for alternating current and his conviction that alternating current was the wave of the future because, unlike direct current, it could be altered to suit the situation. Alternating current, he concluded, was thus far more practical than direct current.

Edison interrupted and told Tesla to stop talking

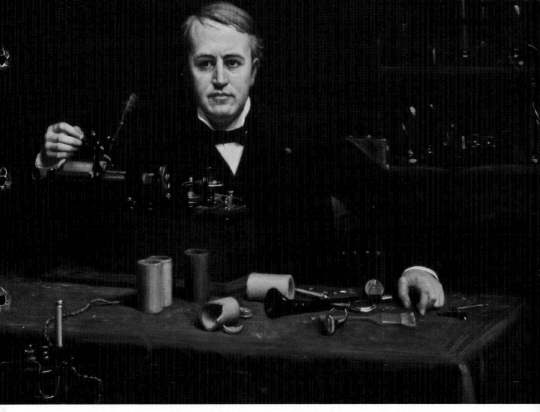

Thomas Alva Edison, circa 1889. *(Courtesy of Art Resource.)*

nonsense about alternating current. It was too dangerous, he said, and America was already set up for direct
current.

Although alternating current was no more dangerous
than direct current, Edison had a lot invested in his
direct-current operations and he was afraid that if alternating current became popular, he would lose a great
deal of money.

But he was not afraid to look for help: Edison asked
Tesla if he was able to fix a ship's lighting plant. Tesla
said he was confident that he could.

Tesla took his tools to the SS *Oregon* and began to
work. The ship's dynamos were in bad shape, full of
breaks and short circuits. He worked through the night

The dynamo room on the SS *Oregon* not long after Tesla's repairs. *(Library of Congress)*

making repairs, with the ship's crew assisting him, and was finished by dawn. On his way back to the shop, he met Edison and a few of his men on the street. He told Edison that the job on the *Oregon* was finished. Edison looked at him in silence, then walked away. Tesla overheard him say to the men, "That is a damn good man."

Edison offered Tesla a job. His shop needed to be redesigned and modified, and he gave Tesla almost complete freedom to accomplish the task. Tesla threw himself into the job, working from ten thirty each morning until five the next morning, reverting back to his strenuous work habits.

Although he kept his faith in alternating current,

Tesla figured out ways Edison's direct-current dynamos could be made more efficient. He convinced Edison that he would save a lot of money if he let him redesign the dynamos. Edison, always interested in saving money, agreed to pay Tesla $50,000 when he completed the work.

It took Tesla a year to redesign the dynamos. When he finished, he went to Edison, reported the job done, and asked when he might be paid the $50,000.

Edison stared at Tesla, open mouthed, then exclaimed, "Tesla, you don't understand American humor!" Edison claimed he had been joking when he offered such a large payment.

Angry and humiliated, Tesla resigned, effective immediately. Edison tried to keep him and offered a ten-dollar per week raise. Tesla refused. Once again he had been cheated out of his salary by an Edison company— and this time by Edison himself.

The relationship between Tesla and Edison was probably doomed from the beginning. They were very different, from their theories on electricity to their personal hygiene. Edison had little formal education and invented by trial and error, eliminating things that did not work until he found one that did. Tesla, on the other hand, was very well educated and approached his work with well-thought-out calculations. Tesla always dressed well, which was a source of pride to him throughout his life. Edison was an ungainly, stooping fellow whose clothes were mismatched and dirty. Tesla was afraid of germs and was therefore fastidious in his hygiene. Edison paid little attention to his own cleanliness.

But their greatest difference was over alternating current. Tesla continued to advocate alternating current as more efficient and safer. Edison saw alternating current as an economic threat. He knew Tesla had a formidable argument and worried that alternating current would render direct current obsolete.

Tesla's time with Edison was not wasted, though. He was able to study Edison at work and to realize that his own plans for producing alternating current were much more advanced than anything Edison had created.

Tesla's growing confidence was boosted when he was approached by a group of investors who offered to help him form a company under his own name—the Tesla Electric Light and Manufacturing Company. Tesla was delighted that an alternating-current system could finally be shown to the world.

His investors insisted, however, that he first improve on the system of arc lights that were then in use. Arc lights, first developed in Europe, used two carbon rods connected to a supply of high voltage electricity, usually a battery. When the rods were drawn apart, an ionized path, or arc, burning at several thousands of degrees, was created between them. This arc heated the ends of the carbon rods, which give off a brilliant light.

Arc light was too bright for homes, but served well in public halls, factories, and railroad yards. There were problems with arc lighting. It was expensive, unsafe, and unreliable. It also flickered annoyingly, because as the carbon rods burned down they needed to be constantly adjusted to maintain the proper spacing so that the arc did not go out. Despite its drawbacks, the appearance of arc lighting showed the public that wide-scale electric lighting was possible.

Tesla began meeting with Lemuel Serrell, a successful and knowledgeable patent attorney who had previously worked for Edison. On March 30, 1885, Tesla applied for his first patent, an improved design of the arc lamp that created uniform light, prevented flickering, and was safer and more economical. The new lamps were a success. The *Electrical Review* took special note of them and featured the Tesla Electric Light Company on the front page of its August 14, 1886, issue.

After Tesla received his patent and the Tesla Electric Light Com-

Tesla's first patent, the electric arc lamp.

N. TESLA.
ELECTRIC ARC LAMP.
No. 335,786.   Patented Feb. 9, 1886.

> ## PATENT SYSTEM
> Patents have been used to protect inventors for thousands of years. The system is simple: a person files a description of her invention or idea with the United States Patent and Trademark Office where it is reviewed to ensure it is original and worthy of a patent. If the patent is granted (a process that can take several years and cost thousands of dollars), it gives the inventor the exclusive right to profit from her invention for a set number of years—usually twenty. It also requires her to allow the Patent Office to publish a public document explaining what her patent is for and how the invention works so that others can benefit from her discovery—even though they can't duplicate it without permission.

pany began making money from it, his investors informed him that they were not interested in producing his alternating-current motor. Tesla was bitterly disappointed and angry. The shoddy treatment did not stop there. As payment for his improvement of arc light, he was promised shares of stock in the new company. Now, they refused to sign over the shares and forced him out of the company altogether.

For the third time, Tesla had been cheated and deceived by Americans. He was broke. During the winter of 1886-1887, he worked as a ditch digger to make ends meet. This was a particular blow to a man who considered himself an intellectual aristocrat. He felt that manual labor made a mockery of his advanced education.

In the spring, Tesla's luck changed. He was contacted by Alfred S. Brown, a famous engineer who worked for the Western Union Telegraph Company. Brown had heard of Tesla, probably through the previous year's article in

A share of the short-lived Tesla Electric Light and Manufacturing Company.

the *Electrical Review*. Brown recognized the advantages of alternating current over direct current and wanted to invest in Tesla's idea, but could not afford to do it alone. He spoke with Charles F. Peck, a prominent lawyer, and tried to convince him to invest in Tesla's alternating-current system. Peck was initially wary of alternating current. But after learning more about it, he was won over. Together, Brown, Peck, and Tesla formed a new company, the Tesla Electric Company. Peck, who had connections to J. Pierpont Morgan, the famous New York financier, provided the bulk of the capital for the company. (Morgan's home was the first in New York to have been lit by Edison's direct current.) Brown provided the company with a laboratory at 89 Liberty Street in lower Manhattan. The company's first patent application was filed on April 30, 1887.

At the age of thirty, Tesla finally had backers who believed in him. He was finally getting to do the work he had dreamed of for so long. Motivated by his success, he relapsed into his old habits and began to work at such a frenzied pace that those around him were soon worried. He sometimes worked until he collapsed. In May of 1887, his friend Anthony Szigeti immigrated to America and began working in the laboratory as Tesla's assistant. He was able to relieve some of the stress.

Szigeti helped Tesla produce three complete systems of alternating-current machinery—for single-phase, two-phase, and three-phase currents—and they experimented with four- and six-phase currents. Single-phase is the current used mainly in homes. Polyphase (more than one phase) currents deliver large amounts of electrical power more efficiently than single-phase currents, and are useful in manufacturing and industry where demand is greater. Tesla produced dynamos for generating the currents, motors for producing power from them, and what came to be known as Tesla coils—transformers for raising and lowering the voltages. News about Tesla's inventions spread quickly.

T. C. Martin, editor of *Electrical World,* visited the laboratory. Thomas Commerford Martin was born the same year as Tesla and came to America from England at the age of twenty-one. He worked for Edison in the late 1870s before moving to the island of Jamaica. In 1883, he returned to New York and became editor of *Operator and Electrical World* (later *Electrical World*), a journal that gained prominence after Edison began contributing articles. In 1884, Martin became vice president of the newly formed American Institute of Electri-

VOLTAGE

A measure of the force with which electricity flows through a wire. Imagine that you are going to spray some leaves off the sidewalk. You connect a hose to the water faucet on the outside of your house. If you just barely turn on the faucet, hardly any water comes out, and the water that does flow out of the hose has very little ability to move leaves. If you turn the faucet on all the way, the force of the water coming out of the hose now is very strong and can move a great many leaves off the sidewalk in a very short period of time. The force of water is called the water pressure. Electricity works the same way, but the force is called voltage instead of pressure. The higher the voltage, the more forcefully the electricity moves through the wires, and the more work it is able to do.

TRANSFORMER

A device that raises and lowers the voltage of electricity. The electricity that is generated from a power plant is at such a high voltage that it would destroy your home at full force. Transformers lower the voltage so that the electricity can be used safely.

cal Engineers (AIEE), and two years later published his first book, *The Electrical Motor and its Applications.* Soon after, he became president of AIEE.

Martin was an opportunist and a charmer who saw in Tesla a vision of the future. He approached Tesla and offered to guide him, socially and otherwise, into the electrical engineering community. Martin arranged for William Anthony, a highly regarded professor of engineering at Cornell University, to come to Tesla's laboratory and test the alternating-current motor. During the visit Anthony, who was soon to become president of the AIEE, tried to convince Tesla to present his alternating-current motor to the society.

Tesla was aware that his invention was worth hundreds of thousands of dollars. He had obtained fourteen of the forty patents available on the various parts of the alternating-current system. However, because of his previous experiences, he doubted the trustworthiness of Americans and was reluctant to present his work to the AIEE for fear his ideas would be stolen.

Tesla sought the advice of his company's patent attorneys. They advised him to seek investors to finance his inventions. By the time of the presentation before the AIEE, negotiations were in the works with prospective investors, including George Westinghouse of Pittsburgh.

On May 15, 1888, Tesla stood before the AIEE membership and presented his paper, "A New System of Alternating Current Motors and Transformers." He carefully explained the theory of alternating current and its

A small model of a Tesla coil. *(Tesla Museum Archives)* practical applica-

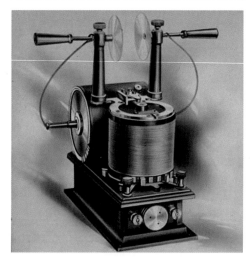

tions. Not only was alternating current more powerful than direct current, it was much more economical. Unlike direct current, which required a powerhouse every mile and copper conduits to be buried under the streets to carry the current, alternating current could travel for hundreds of miles without losing strength, and needed no conduits.

Furthermore, the strength, or voltage, of direct current could not be changed. Tesla explained the Tesla coil, a transformer that could increase the voltage of alternating current as the electricity traveled long distances, then decrease the voltage again for delivery to homes and factories. In Tesla's alternating-current system, a tiny wire could carry a thousand times more electricity than it could in Edison's. Electricity could be generated in one place and used hundreds of miles away. The possibilities of alternating current were endless.

It was a successful presentation. Tesla's place in history as the father of alternating current was assured. But he had also set off a fierce competition with the formidable Thomas Edison. The War of the Currents had begun.

FOUR: THE WAR OF THE CURRENTS

George Westinghouse was already a millionaire when he met Nikola Tesla. Westinghouse had revolutionized railroad travel by inventing air brakes in 1869. He knew that the future was in electricity and founded the Westinghouse Electric Company in 1886. In 1887, Westinghouse Electric had $800,000 in sales. The following year sales jumped to $3 million.

Westinghouse Electric manufactured equipment for the powerhouses that provided electricity for direct-current incandescent lighting. Westinghouse also owned several direct-current distribution stations, but, unlike Edison, he was not convinced direct current was superior to alternating current.

Westinghouse dreamed of sending electricity across the United States. He also wanted to harness the power of Niagara Falls—just as Tesla did—but had not figured out how to do it. When he heard about Tesla's alternating-current motor, he realized that this was what he had been waiting for. Westinghouse was eager to meet the inventor and help market his invention to the world.

George Westinghouse.

The two men developed an instant rapport based on mutual respect. Westinghouse offered to buy all forty of the patents on Tesla's revolutionary new motor for $60,000, including 150 shares of Westinghouse stock, plus $2.50 for each horsepower generated by his invention. Tesla would also have to move to Pittsburgh to work in Westinghouse's plant. Tesla agreed, even though it meant leaving his laboratory in New York and suspending work on the other inventions he had in progress. The chance to manufacture and market his motor was too good an opportunity to pass up.

Soon after arriving at Westinghouse's Pittsburgh plant, Tesla ran into difficulty. American industry had not yet

HORSEPOWER

A unit of measurement of mechanical power. Motors are rated in horsepower, or the amount of work that can be done in a given amount of time. One horsepower is defined as 33,000 foot-pounds of work in one minute. For example, lifting 33,000 pounds a distance of one foot in one minute, or lifting 3,300 pounds ten feet in one minute. The measurement was originally defined by the inventor James Watt, who based it on his calculations about the amount of work one horse could do.

FREQUENCY

The number of times alternating current completes one forth-back-forth motion in one second is called the "frequency," and is measured in cycles per second. In America, the frequency of alternating current most commonly used is 60 cycles per second. Europe and most of the rest of the world use alternating current whose frequency is 50 cycles per second.

standardized the frequency of electric current. Westinghouse's plant used 133-cycle current, but Tesla's motor was designed for 60 cycles. The Westinghouse engineers refused to accommodate Tesla by changing the frequency of the plant's current—which would have been simpler than Tesla trying to adapt his 60-cycle motors to work on 133-cycle current. Months of futile, frustrating, and costly experiments followed.

Thomas Edison was furious when he heard about Westinghouse's arrangement with Tesla. Edison and Westinghouse were already involved in several legal disputes, and Westinghouse's partnership with Tesla made Edison angrier. He began a propaganda campaign

The Westinghouse plant near Pittsburgh, Pennsylvania. *(Library of Congress)*

to convince the public that alternating current was dangerous. Edison's fortune, and his ego, were at stake.

Edison turned his attention to defeating Westinghouse and Tesla. When residents in West Orange, New Jersey, near Edison's huge Menlo Park laboratory, began to notice that their pets were disappearing, they soon discovered the reason. Edison was paying schoolboys twenty-five cents a head for dogs and cats, which he then electrocuted with alternating current in public demonstrations. He dubbed the electrocution process "being Westinghoused." Edison also publicly "Westinghoused" two calves and a horse.

H. P. Brown, an electrical engineer at Columbia University whom Edison recruited to help in the pet electrocution scheme, developed an electric chair that used alternating current. He planned to sell the chairs to prisons for $1,600 apiece—with the stipulation that he be the executioner. The first use of the alternating-current electric chair would be in March 1889 to execute William Kemmler, a man from Buffalo who had axed his mistress to death.

Edison was delighted by the alternating-current electric chair. He hoped it would convince the public that alternating current was far more dangerous than direct current. He did everything he could to aid Brown, even loaning him some of his staff to help build the chair.

Some of the public was outraged when they heard of the upcoming execution by electrocution. In a number of papers and journals, articles reflected concerns and anxiety. One such editorial read: "It is hard to conceive of a more horrible experiment than that which will be made on Kemmler. . . . In a secret place, he will be compelled to go through a process of mental and moral, if not also, bodily torture and nobody can tell how long it will last."

The actual execution was more brutal and gruesome than anyone had imagined. Kemmler was electrocuted for seventeen seconds when, "to the horror of all present, the chest began to heave, foam issued from the mouth, and the man gave every evidence of reviving." One eyewitness claimed he saw Kemmler's spinal cord burst into flames. He had to be electrocuted a second time before he was pronounced dead. Even Edison was disturbed: "I have merely glanced over an account of Kemmler's death, and it is not pleasant reading."

A newspaper artist's portrayal of the gruesome execution of William Kemmler by electric chair.

Edison's propaganda, coupled with the story of Kemmler's execution, sent the public into hysteria. No one wanted anything to do with Tesla's alternating-current induction motor, which required much higher voltages than direct current and was thus, thanks in part to Edison's propaganda, presumed to be more dangerous. Westinghouse tried to distance himself from the hostile public reaction, and his financial backers refused to provide any more money for Tesla's research. They said Tesla had been given enough time to make his induction motor work on 133 cycles. Moreover, they were upset that Westinghouse had agreed to pay Tesla a $2.50 royalty on every horsepower produced. Tesla was devastated when Westinghouse announced that he would stop work on the induction motor.

Tesla returned to New York in 1889, exhausted mentally and physically. Not only was he frustrated by the turn of events in Pittsburgh, but now he was being sued by several people, all claiming to have invented the alternating-current motor. In order to escape the fracas, Tesla traveled to Paris in September 1889 to attend an exposition and see the unveiling of the Eiffel Tower. He had wonderful memories of Paris and was anxious to contact old friends. His spirits were dampened when he learned that Edison would be at the exposition and that he had arranged for a one-acre site to display all his inventions. Edison's exhibit was a huge hit, introducing visitors to, among other things, the phonograph.

A view of the base of the Eiffel Tower and the exposition grounds in 1889. *(Library of Congress)*

From Paris, Tesla went to Croatia. After visiting his mother and sisters, he returned to New York. Reinvigorated, he began work in his new laboratory, which took up the entire fourth floor of a six-story building at 33-35 South Fifth Avenue (now West Broadway). He made his home at the Astor House, an elegant hotel in the center of the city.

Edison, meanwhile, continued to tour Europe, receiving accolades wherever he visited. He was honored by Queen Marguerite in Venice and King Humbert in Rome. In Germany he met with Hermann von Helmholtz, a doctor who had abandoned medicine in favor of studying electrodynamics. At Heidelberg, he demonstrated his phonograph before a crowd of 15,000. Edison's greatest thrill came when he was invited to attend a dinner given by Buffalo Bill, who was touring Europe with his Wild West Show.

Edison continued on to London and there met with

The famous Astor House. *(Library of Congress)*

an increasingly stark reality. News of alternating current had spread across Europe, and despite Edison's best efforts to make alternating current frightening, the European public was discovering its benefits. Everyone was talking about Tesla. Fearing for his financial future, Edison put even more effort into his campaign against alternating current.

Although George Westinghouse was no longer working to produce Tesla's alternating-current motor, he still firmly believed in the superiority of alternating current over direct current. With help from Professor Anthony at Cornell and other respected scientists, he continued to educate the public about its safety. Tesla, operating on the idea that seeing is believing, put on remarkable public and private demonstrations to show that alternating current was less risky than direct current.

When it became clear that he was losing ground, Edison's associates urged him to stop his negative campaign. It was costing him money; his finances were in a shambles. But Edison refused to give up. He was a stubborn man who would rather get ahead than give in.

FIVE: GOING WIRELESS

By the early 1890s, Tesla had become a well-known figure in engineering circles. He wrote a book, edited by T. C. Martin, titled *The Inventions, Researches and Writings of Nikola Tesla* and containing material on alternating-current motors, the rotating magnetic field, polyphase systems, and more. It was a useful book that many engineers read and it helped to cement his reputation.

Tesla was not always treated with respect or given due credit for his inventions, however. His peers by now recognized that alternating current would power the future, and many of them rushed to claim that Tesla's ideas had been theirs first. Many of them had experimented with alternating current, but none had predated Tesla's revolutionary rotating magnetic field.

One of Tesla's most disappointing associations was with a peer and fellow countryman, Michael Pupin. Born in Idvor, a Serbian town north of Belgrade, Pupin immigrated to the United States in 1874. He had an intense interest in electricity. He entered Columbia College in New York City in 1878, graduating with honors in 1884. He then went to Germany and received a doctorate in physics from the University of Berlin, and returned to the United States to become an instructor in the electrical engineering department at Columbia College.

Pupin greatly admired Tesla's work but he got caught up in the controversy about who actually invented the alternating-current system. Pupin became friendly with Elihu Thomson of the Thomson-Houston Electric Company. Thomson's company was facing financial ruin unless it started using the more efficient alternating-

Michael Pupin *(front right)* with Tesla's other rival, Thomas Edison *(front left)*.

current machinery. But Tesla's patents, owned by Westinghouse, prohibited them from doing so. Thomson had come close to inventing an alternating-current system at the same time Tesla received his patent, and therefore resented Tesla.

The three men came together at a three-day AIEE symposium held in May 1891. Tesla was invited to speak, and many of the engineers in attendance were inspired by his mesmerizing words and demonstrations of new principles of electricity. He produced light by the use of vacuum tubes, presenting the principles of fluorescent and neon light. He showed the world that alternating current is safe when used correctly. Tesla went on to explain to the spellbound audience that energy exists everywhere and that it can be neither created nor destroyed. He predicted many magnificent future developments, such as pictures broadcast through the air (what would later become television) and the wireless transmission of power.

In the audience, Thomson and Pupin tried to distract Tesla while he was giving his speech. Tesla later told a Serbian reporter, "While I was lecturing, Mr. Pupin, with his friends, interrupted by whistling, and I had difficulty quieting down the . . . audience." Pupin later wrote Tesla to apologize and asked to see a demonstration of the alternating-current polyphase motor. Tesla did not respond and from that point on avoided Pupin. Though Pupin wanted to reconcile with Tesla, the two men remained estranged. Tesla had learned not to trust even those who claimed to be his friends.

As Tesla's fame and popularity grew, so did his competition's determination. On February 17, 1892, the *Electrical Engineer* announced that the Edison General Electric Company was merging with the Thomson-Houston Company. The new firm was to be called General Electric. The man behind the merger was J. Pierpont Morgan, who had previously taken over control of Thomson-Houston. Westinghouse would now have an even bigger and more formidable competitor. But General Electric still could not legally generate alternating current because Westinghouse held the patents.

Tesla worked on, mostly oblivious to the outside world. He had become obsessed with what he called wireless telephone—later to be known as wireless, and then radio. For over a year he labored in vain to produce the radio. He went without adequate sleep for months, and finally collapsed into a deep sleep. When he awoke, he was shocked to discover that he had no memory of his life except early infancy, although he was able to recall complex mathematical formulae and passages of text from his research. He refused to see a physician and decided to cure himself.

Each night he concentrated on his early life, and gradually more of his memories returned. He noticed that his mother was prominent in all his memories, and he developed an urgency to see her. One night while concentrating on reconstructing his early memories, Tesla had a vision of himself in the Hotel de la Paix in Paris being handed a note that said his mother was dying.

Word of Tesla's genius and accomplishments had by this time spread to Europe, and he had received many invitations to speak before European scientific societies. Tesla decided to accept invitations to speak in London and Paris, and then go to Gospic to see his family. His lecture to the electrical engineers in London was highly acclaimed, and he was invited to speak before the prestigious Royal Society of Great Britain. Attended by the elite of the scientific world, the Royal Society embraced Tesla and hailed him as a genius.

Leaving London in April 1892, Tesla hurried to Paris. Following several lectures, he returned exhausted to his room in the Hotel de la Paix. As he began to relax, he heard a knock at the door. There stood a messenger with a telegram. Tesla's mother was dying.

Tesla hurried to the train station and boarded a train for Croatia. His three sisters and his Uncle Petar greeted

Tesla's three sisters. *From left to right:* Milka, Angelina, and Marica. *(Tesla Museum Archives)*

him at his boyhood home. He entered his mother's bedroom and found her in agony. He was able to spend a few hours with her and then, exhausted emotionally and physically, he went to bed. He later wrote, "As I lay helpless there, I thought that if my mother died while I was away from her bedside that she would surely give me a sign."

Early the next morning, in a dream, Tesla saw "a cloud carrying angelic figures of marvelous beauty, one of whom gazed upon me lovingly and gradually assumed the features of my mother. The appearance slowly floated across the room and vanished, and I was awakened by an indescribably sweet song of many voices. In that instant a certitude, which no words can express, came upon me that my mother had just died. And that was true."

Tesla was ill for several weeks following his mother's death. While recuperating, he took walks in the mountains he loved to roam as a boy. On one walk he watched an approaching thunderstorm and noticed that the rain began to pour following a particularly magnificent flash of lightning. He concluded there was a cause and effect in operation and wondered if lightning was the trigger that started the rain. If that was true, he hypothesized that he could artificially produce lightning and control the weather, irrigating deserts and creating lakes and rivers. This idea would become his new obsession.

Tesla returned to America in August 1892. He made scientific history again in the spring of 1893 when, in

Tesla lecturing on and demonstrating high-frequency currents and radio transmission in 1893. *(Tesla Wardenclyffe Project Archives)*

a lecture in St. Louis at the National Electric Light Association, he described in detail the principles of radio transmission and made the first public demonstration ever of radio communication. On stage he set up two groups of equipment: the transmitter group and the receiver group. The transmitter group was composed of a high-voltage transformer connected to a condenser, a spark gap, a Tesla coil, and a wire running up to the ceiling. In the receiver group thirty feet away was an identical wire hanging from the ceiling, a condenser, and a Tesla coil. In this group, however, instead of a spark gap, there was a tube that would light up when voltage was applied. No wires connected the transmitter and the receiver.

The transformer in the transmitter group received its energy from an electric power line connected to a switch. When the switch was closed, the transformer sprang to life, a spark jumped audibly across the spark gap, and an invisible electromagnetic field radiated energy into space from the transmitter antenna wire. The antenna on the receiving apparatus picked up a radio frequency generated by the transmitter, causing the tube to glow.

Tesla had successfully demonstrated the principle of the radio. He described his wireless system in a lecture that was published in 1893, translated into ten languages, and distributed around the world. This worldwide distribution of his discoveries and inventions would soon come back to haunt him.

The 1893 Chicago World's Fair, also called the Columbian Exposition, commemorated the 400th anniversary of Columbus's first voyage to America. Billed as "The World of Tomorrow," the fair was to be the world's first illuminated by electricity. General Electric (GE) and Westinghouse Electric bid for the right to provide the lighting. GE offered to do the job for one million dollars; Westinghouse said it would do it for half that. Much of GE's proposed expenses were tied to the amount of copper wire that would be necessary for direct-current power. Westinghouse proposed a much more efficient alternating-current system and was awarded the contract. He was determined to prove once and for all that alternating current was safe.

Edison was once again furious. In retaliation, he legally prevented Westinghouse from using his one-piece incandescent light bulb. Westinghouse hurriedly designed and manufactured a two-piece "stopper" lamp that saved the day.

An overview of the Chicago World's Fair. *(Library of Congress)*

Tens of thousands of people attended the opening day on May 1, 1893. The fair covered 633 acres. Visitors marveled at displays in two hundred buildings and were fascinated by one of the newest inventions—the Ferris wheel. Fifty cents—twice the cost of admission to the fair—bought two revolutions on the giant wheel.

Of all the buildings at the exposition, the Great Hall of Electricity was the most popular. Electricity had been introduced to home use with Edison's light bulb only fourteen years before, but other inventions using electricity were being developed and put into widespread use. Exhibits demonstrated electricity's practical and entertainment value, including all the household electrical appliances of the period—electric lamps, elevators, fans, sewing machines, burglar alarms, stoves, laundry machines, and irons.

After sunset on opening day, the president of the United States, Grover Cleveland, pushed a button and

100,000 incandescent lamps illuminated the fairgrounds. This "City of Light" was the work of Tesla, Westinghouse, and twelve new one-thousand-horsepower alternating-current generators located in the Hall of Machinery. Visitors were in awe. Such a spectacle of light had never been seen anywhere in the world. To the twenty-seven million visitors over the next six months, it was clear that alternating current was the future. From that point on, more than eighty percent of all electrical devices ordered in the United States were designed to run on alternating current.

For all Tesla's successes, one goal was always most important to him. He loved the freedom and opportunity that America offered, and he wanted to become a citizen.

Tesla's spectacular "City of Light" at the Columbian Exposition in Chicago in 1893. *(Westinghouse Archives)*

On July 30, 1893, he was granted citizenship of the United States of America. He often told his friends that his American citizenship meant more to him than any scientific honor. The medals or honorary degrees he accrued in his life were tossed into a drawer. His certificate of naturalization was kept in a safe in his office.

SIX: PECULIARITIES

T. C. Martin kept his promise to Tesla to introduce him to the electrical world and make him famous. He had also promised to introduce Tesla to society. Martin knew many of the most prominent people of the day. Among them was Robert Underwood Johnson, associate editor of *Century* magazine. Though not particularly wealthy, Johnson and his wife, Katharine, were socially ambitious and surrounded themselves with the rich and famous. They were gracious hosts and often entertained such guests as Theodore Roosevelt, Mark Twain, sculptor August Saint-Gaudens, naturalist John Muir, children's activist Mary Mapes Dodge, author Rudyard Kipling, architect Stanford White, and composer Ignace Paderewski. The composer Antonin Dvorak also spent time with the Johnsons during the two years he was in the United States, during which time he composed the *New World Symphony*.

Mark Twain had met Tesla in 1888. Afterward, he wrote in his famous notebook, "I have just seen the drawings & description of an electrical machine lately patented by a Mr. Tesla, & sold to the Westinghouse Company, which will revolutionize the whole electric business of the world. It is the most valuable patent since the telephone." Twain was in awe of Tesla's genius. The two men became friends after Tesla told Twain of the profound effect Twain's books had on his illness while he was a boy in Croatia.

In mid-December 1893, Martin suggested to Johnson that he do an article for *Century* on Nikola Tesla. Johnson was familiar with electricians. During the 1880s, when

Mark Twain in Tesla's lab. *(Tesla Wardenclyffe Project Archives)*

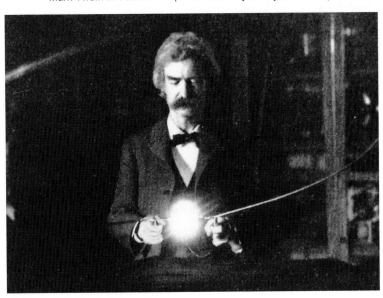

he was a reporter for *Scribner's Monthly*, he had inter-viewed Edison at his laboratory. Now he welcomed the chance to meet Tesla. He invited Martin to dinner and suggested he bring Tesla along.

On the appointed evening, Martin and Tesla arrived at 327 Lexington Avenue and were greeted by Robert and Katharine and their two teenage children, Agnes and Owen. Robert and Katharine were surprised by Tesla. Nearly six feet four, he weighed no more than 140 pounds. Katharine was entranced by the thin, gaunt Tesla and pitied his haggard appearance. Following a lively dinner conversation, during which Tesla told his hosts about his experiments and his recent European speaking tour, Katharine invited Tesla to join them for a good Christmas meal, just a few weeks away.

Tesla replied that he received all the nourishment he needed from his laboratory. "I know I am completely worn out," he said, "and yet I cannot stop my work. These experiments of mine are so important, so beautiful, so fascinating, that I can hardly tear myself away from them to eat, and when I try to sleep I think about them constantly. I expect I shall go on until I break down altogether."

After dessert, Tesla invited the party to accompany him to his laboratory. He warned them to prepare them-selves for a surprise or two. They were awed by what they saw. The lab was filled with bizarre equipment. Tesla drew the heavy black curtains across the windows, making the room pitch black, and put on a spectacular demon-

Tesla with one of the famous wireless bulbs. *(Tesla Museum Archives)*

stration. He gave a light bulb to each person and filled the room with electric vibrations until the bulbs in their hands began to glow. Each person was bombarded by electricity, yet no one was hurt—as long as the voltage was low, alternating current was perfectly safe.

Robert Johnson, holding a loop with an incandescent lamp, with Tesla in his lab. *(Tesla Museum Archives)*

After the demonstration, Katharine Johnson was even more fascinated by her new acquaintance. A few days after their first meeting, she sent Tesla a bouquet of beautiful winter flowers. In response, Tesla wrote to Robert Johnson, "I have never . . . received flowers, and they produced on me a curious effect." Always more comfortable with animals or machines than with people, Tesla was not quite sure how to respond to the Johnsons. But they persisted and began what would become a long and intimate friendship. Tesla became a regular dinner guest at their home, and he in turn treated them to dinner at Delmonico's, a landmark New York restaurant.

Robert was fascinated by Tesla's heritage and began reading Serbian poetry Tesla translated for him. One of their favorites was a ballad by Zmaj Jovanovich called "Luka Filipov." The poem tells of a warrior, Luka Filipov, who fought in a fierce battle in Montenegro in 1874. The Johnsons loved the poem, and Robert became known to Tesla as his dear Luka and Katharine as Mrs. Filipov.

Katharine Johnson was an intelligent, poised, and playful woman who longed for excitement and intellectual stimulation. Tesla became a kind of trophy to her. She loved to show him off to her friends. A passionate woman, it's likely that her feelings for Tesla were stronger than their platonic friendship revealed. Tesla once told a friend that Katharine tried to seduce him one day

Tesla's friend and admirer, New York socialite Katharine Johnson. *(Tesla Museum Archives)*

when Robert was not at home. Ever the gentleman, and out of respect for Robert, Tesla declined and left the house.

Tesla was tall and handsome, and had a charismatic personality. Robert Johnson once described him as a man of "distinguished sweetness, sincerity, modesty, refinement, generosity and force." Always impeccably dressed, he usually wore a black Prince Albert coat and a derby hat, even to his laboratory, unless a public demonstration demanded that he don more formal wear. His handkerchiefs were white silk rather than the usual linen, and he always wore gloves, usually gray suede. He considered himself to be the best-dressed man on Fifth Avenue in New York, and told Dorothy F. Skerritt, his secretary for many years, that he intended to remain so. Skerritt said that even in his old age, Tesla cut an impressive figure: "From under protruding eyebrows, his deep-set, steel gray, soft, yet piercing eyes, seemed to read your innermost thoughts . . . his face glowed with almost ethereal radiance. . . . His genial smile and nobility of bearing always denoted the gentlemanly characteristics that were so ingrained in his soul."

Although women were attracted to him, Tesla never married. He had made a conscious choice between women and his career, and believed that romantic attachments would complicate his life and deter him from his work. A newspaper article once quoted him as saying, "I believe that a writer or a musician should marry. They gain inspiration that leads to finer achievement. But an inventor has so intense a nature, with so much in it of wild, passionate quality that, in giving himself to a woman, he would give up everything, and so take everything from his chosen field. It is a pity, too; sometimes we feel so lonely."

Despite his choice to remain unmarried, Tesla admired women. Marguerite Merington, whom he met at the Johnsons', especially intrigued him. A statuesque and enchanting woman, Merington was a playwright, author, and composer. Her accomplishments confirmed Tesla's belief that some day women would fight for equality with men and that "the female mind has demonstrated a capacity for all the mental acquirements and achievements of men, and as generations ensue . . . the average woman will be as well educated as the average man, and then better educated, for the dormant faculties of her brain will be stimulated into an activity that will be all the more intense because of centuries of repose. Women will . . . startle civilization with their progress."

Though Tesla did have friendships and a social life, he also suffered from a number of phobias that hampered his interactions. He was terrified of germs and refused to shake hands. When someone approached, he usually held his hands behind his back. This led to several embarrassing moments as the visitor stretched his hand out and Tesla did not reciprocate. On the rare occasion when a visitor to his lab did succeed in shaking his hand, Tesla was so upset that he could not concentrate on the conversation. He usually ended the visit quickly so he could rush to the washroom and scrub his hands.

Whenever he spied workmen eating their lunches with dirty hands, he became nauseous. He even threw out his gloves after wearing them only two or three times.

Tesla had a particular loathing for earrings, especially pearls, and was unable to speak to women who wore them. In fact, anything smooth and round troubled him. It took several years for him to get comfortable with billiard balls so that he could enjoy the game. Like many people who suffer from such disorders, Tesla obsessively catalogued his symptoms. He claimed that the smell of camphor caused him intense discomfort, and that if he dropped little squares of paper into a dish of water, he got a terrible taste in his mouth. He counted every step he took, a disorder called arithmomania. Before he ate, he had to mentally calculate the cubic volume of his food. If he failed to do this, he could not enjoy his meal. He also refused to touch the hair of any person and believed that three was a magic number.

Tesla's employees were fiercely loyal to him. He adhered strictly to an unchanging work schedule. He arrived at his office exactly at noon and insisted that one of his secretaries meet him at the door to take his hat, cane, and gloves. All the drapes were drawn across the windows to simulate nighttime. They were opened only in the event of a lightning storm. Tesla would then lie on his black couch and watch the sky. His secretaries reported that he had to be alone during these storms, but that they could hear him talking to himself rapturously about the lightning.

Nikola Tesla in 1895 at age thirty-nine. *(Library of Congress)*

Musicians, writers, actors, poets, and foreign governments sought out Tesla. He was called a wizard, a visionary, a prophet, and the greatest scientist of all time. But he had many detractors. Waldemar Kaempffert, science editor of the *New York Times*, branded him a "medieval practitioner of black arts." Tesla also had a following among practitioners of the occult, who claimed he had been born on Venus and arrived on Earth on the wings of a large white dove. Tesla did not appreciate these fans because they gave fuel to the fire of his enemies, many of whom were jealous fellow scientists.

Despite his popularity, Tesla spent most of his time alone, a condition he preferred because it gave him greater control over his environment. He lived in hotels most of his life and ate in their dining rooms. His good friend John J. O'Neill wrote: "He required that the table he used in the dining room of his hotel be not used by others. A fresh tablecloth was required for every meal. He also required that a stack of eighteen napkins be placed on the left side of the table." He chose eighteen because it was evenly divisible by three—Tesla's magic number. As each item of silverware and each dish were brought to him—he required that they be sterilized by heat before leaving the kitchen—he would pick each up with a napkin, and use another napkin to clean it. He would then drop both napkins on the floor. Even for a simple meal, he ran through the full stock of napkins.

Tesla abhorred flies, and one alighting on his table meant everything had to be removed and the meal started over again.

John J. O'Neill went on to describe Tesla's culinary peculiarities: "In Tesla's earlier years, for dinner, he greatly enjoyed fine thick steaks, preferably the filet mignon, and it was not unusual for him to consume two or three at a sitting. Later his preference turned to lamb, and he would frequently order a roast saddle of it. While the saddle was usually large enough to serve a party of several persons, as a rule he ate of it only the central portion of the tenderloin. A crown of baby lamb chops was another favorite dish. He also relished roast squab with nut stuffing. In fowl, however, his choice was roast duck. He required that it be roasted under a smothering of celery stalks. This method of preparing the duck was of his own devising. He very often made it the central motif around which a dinner was designed when entertaining friends, and on such occasions he would go to the kitchen [of the hotel] to superintend its preparation. Duck so prepared was nevertheless delicious. Of the duck he ate only the meat on either side of the breast bone."

Later in his life Tesla gave up meat. His health was another thing to obsess over. He smoked heavily for many years, but when one of his sisters became ill, she promised him that she would get well if he gave up smoking. He did and she recovered. He drank coffee until he decided that it was bad for his health. He had great difficulty giving it up, however, and for years insisted that a fresh cup of coffee be poured for him at each meal so he could savor the aroma.

Tesla also considered tea and hot cocoa to be bad for his health, but he found whiskey to be very beneficial. He believed that many of his ancestors had lived long

SEVEN: ALTERNATING CURRENT

In 1894, Tesla began experimenting with high-frequency electromagnetic radiation. Twenty years before, in England, James Clerk Maxwell had hypothesized that light is energy and that, because the frequency of energy waves can be changed, there must be different kinds of electromagnetic radiation in the universe. Tesla took Maxwell's idea further by trying to find a way to produce high-frequency radiation. He invented a new cone-shaped coil that could produce one million volts of high-frequency electricity. By 1895, he was ready to transmit a radio signal a distance of fifty miles. He believed that the step after that was to signal other planets. Tesla firmly believed that life existed beyond the planet Earth.

Tesla planned to transmit messages from his laboratory to receiving equipment on a steamboat on the

> ### ELECTROMAGNETIC RADIATION
> Radiation is energy that travels through space and spreads out as it goes, and is made up of "waves" of different lengths. The universe produces a spectrum, or range, of electromagnetic radiation. From the longest rays to the shortest, the electromagnetic spectrum is comprised of radio waves, infrared rays, visible light, ultraviolet rays, x-rays, and gamma rays. "Visible light" is the electromagnetic waves that enter our eyes and stimulate the retina to transform the waves into information that our brains can "see." Humans are unable to see other forms of electromagnetic radiation. The longest rays also have the lowest frequencies—the highest frequency belongs to gamma rays.

Hudson River. Before he could conduct his experiment, however, tragedy struck. On March 13, 1895, his laboratory burned to the ground.

It was a shattering blow. T. C. Martin wrote in *Engineering Magazine* in April 1895, "Two tottering brick walls and the yawning jaws of a somber cavity aswim with black water and oil were all that could be seen [that] morning . . . of a laboratory which to all who had visited it was one of the most interesting spots on earth. . . . Perhaps the most painful loss of all is the destruction of Mr. Tesla's notes and papers. His memory is all right . . . but [it will take years] for the inventor to recreate his ongoing investigations . . . [Nevertheless,] while the ashes of his hopes lay hot . . . Tesla was at work again with clenched determination."

Thomas Edison implied that the fire was caused by Tesla's alternating-current motor, though there was no evidence to indicate that was the case. It had actually

FRUITS OF GENIUS WERE SWEPT AWAY.

By a Fire the Noted Electrician, Nicola Tesla, Loses Mechanisms of Inestimable Value.

INVENTIONS IN THE RUINS.

The Workshop Where He Evolved Ideas That Startled Electricians Entirely Destroyed.

YEARS OF LABOR LOST.

This *New York Herald* article from March 14, 1895, reported the devastation Tesla suffered from the laboratory fire.

started below his lab in a dry-cleaning establishment. Still, the accident was a setback that plunged Tesla into a depression. He had no insurance, and the cost of rebuilding was prohibitive. He was still receiving royalties from patents he had sold in Europe and small payments from the Westinghouse corporation, but he needed to raise additional funds in order to rebuild his laboratory. He contacted Albert Schmid of Westinghouse and asked him to send him new equipment. Schmid did, but Tesla was surprised when Westinghouse billed him for the equipment lost in the fire, which Westinghouse had loaned to him. The company also billed him for the new equipment, putting Tesla even deeper in debt.

Desperate for a place to work, Tesla turned to the one man whom he knew had the equipment to allow him to continue his experiments—Thomas Edison. Though Tesla was his rival, Edison had sympathy for his misfortune. He allowed Tesla to use his laboratory. The press had a field day with the news that the two rivals were working side by side. The *Troy Press* of New York inquired in an article, "Who Is King, Edison or Tesla?" The two inventors were dubbed the "Twin Wizards of Electricity."

In May 1895, at the National Electrical Exposition in Philadelphia, Tesla's alternating current was transmitted a distance of five hundred miles for the first time. Alexander Graham Bell, also at the exposition, later proclaimed, "This long distance transmission of electric power was the most important discovery of electric science that had been made for many years."

Tesla was equally gratified. "I am now convinced beyond any question that it is possible to transmit electricity . . . by water power . . . over a distance of five hundred miles at half the cost of generation by steam [or coal] . . . I am willing to stake my reputation and my life upon this declaration."

Tesla soon saw another of his dreams come true. Americans had been envisioning Niagara Falls as a source of power since the first sawmill was built there in 1725. The International Niagara Commission was established in 1891 to explore the best means of harnessing Niagara Falls, and had held a contest for the best powerhouse design, with a prize of $3,000. Twenty submissions were entered, but not one won the reward.

Neither Westinghouse nor Edison had entered the contest. Westinghouse was offended that the prize was so small, saying that the commission was "trying to get one hundred thousand dollars worth of information for three thousand dollars."

Lord Kelvin, the famous English scientist, was chairman of the commission. He opposed alternating current, believing it to be unsafe. He wrote a note to the others on the commission: "I trust you will avoid the gigantic mistake of alternating current." However, when Lord Kelvin visited the Chicago World's Fair and witnessed alternating current in action, he changed his mind. He and the commission approached Westinghouse and asked him to use alternating current to harness the falls. When Tesla heard the news, he was thrilled, for it was his inventions that Westinghouse would use to produce electricity from Niagara Falls—just as he had dreamed as a boy.

The Niagara Falls project was financed by some of the wealthiest men in America: J. Pierpont Morgan, John Jacob Astor III, Lord Rothschild, and W. K. Vanderbilt. Though Tesla was eminently confident that the project would work, because he already saw it working perfectly in his mind, his investors were nervous. Nothing of this magnitude had ever been tried before.

KINETIC ENERGY
The energy found in a moving object. The motion of a rock tumbling down a hill is an example of kinetic energy.

MECHANICAL ENERGY
The energy something has because it is in motion (a moving bicycle) or because it has stored potential energy (a drawn bow).

Overseen by Edward Dean Adams, president of the Cataract Construction Company, river water just above the falls was diverted into 140-foot-long shafts placed vertically into the ground. Within each shaft, the force of the falling water turned the blades of a turbine, which transformed the kinetic energy of the moving water into mechanical energy. The mechanical energy activated generators in a powerhouse, which pro-duced electrical energy in the form of polyphase alternating current.

On November 16, 1896, the switch at Niagara Falls was thrown and the first electricity reached Buffalo, New York, just seconds later. The first thousand horse-power produced were claimed by the street railway com-pany in Buffalo, but residents had already ordered five thousand more from the local power company. Within a few years there were ten generators at Niagara Falls, and some were used to make electricity for New York City. Lights blazed on Broadway and in homes; electric trol-leys and subways rumbled throughout the city. Soon

Opposite: Tesla had a lifelong dream of harnessing the tremendous power of Niagara Falls. *(Library of Congress)*

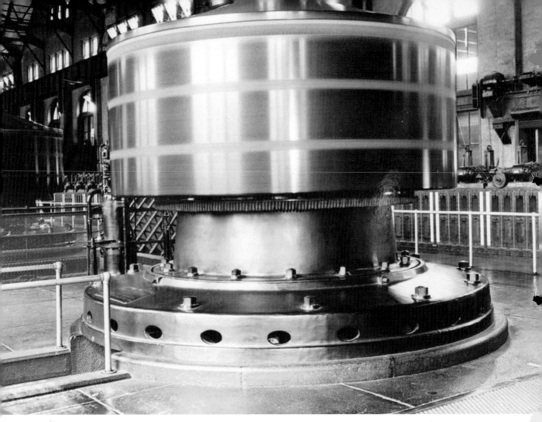

One of Tesla's generators at the Edward Dean Adams station at Niagara Falls. *(Library of Congress)*

even Edison's direct-current systems would be converted to alternating current.

The War of the Currents was over. However, the rivalry had taken a serious toll on the Westinghouse corporation, which had spent millions of dollars trying to prove that alternating current was superior to direct current. Westinghouse was on the brink of financial collapse.

J. P. Morgan was still interested in finding ways to profit from electric power. To do so, he would first have to acquire control of the Tesla patents in order to legally utilize his technology. He would prefer to buy them outright from Westinghouse, but if necessary he would seize them any way he could.

Charles Coffin, CEO of GE, approached George Westinghouse about the possibility of a merger between Westinghouse Electric and General Electric. When Westinghouse rejected the offer, Coffin retaliated by spreading rumors about Westinghouse's finances, saying in print that he was close to financial ruin. Westinghouse stocks crashed on Wall Street.

Westinghouse told Tesla of his dilemma. He reminded Tesla of the clause in his contract that promised Tesla $2.50 for every horsepower produced. He already owed Tesla twelve million dollars. Westinghouse then asked Tesla to help him save the company by voiding the contract. Tesla asked Westinghouse what he would do if he refused.

"In that event you would have to deal with the bankers, for I would no longer have any power in the situation," Westinghouse responded.

Tesla continued, "And if I give up the contract, will you save your company and retain control? You will

---

SUBWAY

Work on the first electric subway in the United States began in Manhattan, New York, in March 1900. William Barclay Parsons, chief engineer on the project, faced incredible challenges in designing and building an underground railway in a densely populated urban area. On October 27, 1904, the first passengers boarded the subway. The original line was 9.1 miles long and consisted of twenty-eight stations. It took twenty-six minutes for the first train to go along Broadway from City Hall to the final stop at 145th Street. The subway contributed to great social and economic growth in New York City. Today 4.5 million people ride the New York City subways every day.

proceed with your plans to give my polyphase system to the world?"

"I believe your polyphase system is the greatest discovery in the field of electricity," said Westinghouse. He said that no matter what happened to his own company, he intended to continue with his plans to put the homes and factories of the entire country on alternating current.

Tesla thought for a moment about the gratitude he had for the one man who had initially believed in his alternating-current system and made its production possible. Tesla was convinced that even greater inventions lay ahead. He tore his contract to pieces, thereby saving the Westinghouse Electric Corporation.

In voiding his contract with Westinghouse, Tesla not only relinquished the millions of dollars already owed him, he also forfeited the many millions that he would have earned in the future. Tearing up the contract was an act of generosity and friendship. Even though the contract was now void, Tesla believed that Westinghouse would acknowledge his contribution to the company with a handsome financial reward. He was doomed to be disappointed. While Westinghouse continued to make millions, Tesla received little and would eventually slip into poverty, from which he would never emerge.

EIGHT: MASTER OF LIGHTNING

By 1897, Tesla had invented and received patents on the equipment needed for generating, modulating, storing, transmitting, and receiving radio signals. But competition to create the new technologies was fierce, and Tesla had reason to believe that at least one man was pirating his ideas and his equipment. Following the translation and worldwide publication of Tesla's lecture on wireless transmission in 1893, the young Italian Guglielmo Marconi showed up in London with wireless equipment designed exactly as described by Tesla. When challenged, Marconi denied that he had ever heard of Tesla's system. In July 1896, Marconi successfully transmitted radio waves through walls and over distances of several miles. But when he applied for a patent, it was denied because he was using ideas already patented by Tesla.

Guglielmo Marconi. *(Library of Congress)*

Undaunted, Marconi made a bid for public attention by planning to transmit wireless signals across the English Channel. His ploy worked, garnering him a new partner in Thomas Edison. Though Tesla had demonstrated wireless transmission years earlier, it had always been to small private audiences in lecture halls. He was no longer interested in grand demonstrations, such as the one he had planned before his laboratory burned down. Tesla now became obsessed with finding a way to transmit wireless power.

Tesla believed that the Earth emits a frequency that could be used as a carrier wave through the ionosphere (part of the Earth's upper atmosphere). He thought it would be possible to generate energy from any place on Earth and transmit it through the ionosphere to any other place, where it could be received and converted into power. He needed money to test his idea.

At the time, Tesla's major financial backer was Edward Dean Adams, who had financed the Niagara Falls project. But Adams was not interested in Tesla's wireless

WIRELESS POWER

Tesla's concept of wireless power is still being explored today. Converting electricity into microwaves means it can be beamed around the world and then reconstituted at its destination. While current applications of wireless power remain limited (for example, a small pad that can charge mobile electronic devices without connecting wires), the possibilities are endless. Wireless power would eliminate the need for complicated, expensive, and inefficient infrastructure. It would allow poor or remote areas to enjoy the benefits of electricity. Wireless power could be sent around the world. When it was dark in Australia, people there could draw power produced by solar panels in the United States, and vice versa. Tesla's dream of free electricity for everyone remains a dream—but also a possibility.

This diagram, explaining Tesla's ideas for wireless power, was printed in the February 1919 issue of the *Electrical Experimenter*.

power scheme. Tesla then appealed to Westinghouse, who also turned him away. Westinghouse was getting rich off Tesla's alternating-current motor and was expanding it to other applications, such as electric subway trains. Tesla believed he should receive royalties for this new venture, but Westinghouse made it clear that Tesla would receive nothing beyond what he had already gotten. By this time, Westinghouse and General Electric had come to a tenuous truce and were cooperating on a few ventures. Now, a second big corporation, General Electric, would benefit from Tesla's ideas.

NATURAL FREQUENCY

Everything in the universe—including you—is made up of little particles so tiny you cannot see them with an ordinary microscope. These particles are called atoms, and atoms are made up of even smaller particles—protons, neutrons, and electrons. Electrons are constantly orbiting the center, or nucleus, of the atom, much like the Earth and other planets orbit the sun. Because electrons are constantly moving, everything in the universe vibrates—rocks, trees, buildings— even you. Although the vibrations are so small that you cannot feel or see them, they are constantly moving at a steady pace, or natural frequency. If an object is inundated with wavelengths that match its natural frequency, that object can be destroyed. It's true that singers can shatter glass—not by singing badly but by hitting and holding a note that matches the natural frequency of a glass long enough to overwhelm it. Since every glass will have a different natural frequency, depending upon its composition, it would take different notes to shatter different glasses. Natural frequency is of great concern to builders. The Tacoma Narrows Bridge was famously destroyed when its natural frequency was matched by wind gusts of such duration that the bridge broke itself apart. In medical applications, natural frequency can be used to destroy kidney stones, which can help avoid painful operations. Doctors can target the kidney stones with sound waves until the stones' natural frequency is found and they are destroyed.

OSCILLATOR

An oscillator is an electrical device that produces certain frequencies. The word "oscillate" means to swing back and forth, like a pendulum, or to vary between two extremes.

Despite these setbacks, Tesla continued with his experiments. One day he placed one of his mechanical oscillators on a support beam. He adjusted the frequency of the oscillator to match the frequency of the support beam. As the oscillator began to hum, he was distracted by something in his laboratory and turned his attention momentarily away. The device continued to vibrate against the beam with precisely timed pulses, magnifying the frequency of the beam and thus the vibrations. Soon the building began to shake, then the ground outside and other buildings nearby. Frantic citizens called the fire department. The only thing that saved the building from collapse was Tesla, who quickly grabbed a hammer and destroyed the oscillator.

Tesla later told a reporter that he once found a building under construction in the Wall Street district. The building had a steel framework and was about ten stories high. Tesla clamped his oscillator to one of the beams and adjusted the frequency until it matched that of the beam. "In a few minutes I could feel the beam trembling. Gradually, the trembling increased in intensity and extended throughout the whole great mass of steel. Finally, the structure began to creak and weave, and the steel workers came to the ground panic-stricken, believing there had been an earthquake. Rumors spread that the building was about to fall, and the police reserves were called out. Before anything serious happened, I took off the vibrator, put it in my pocket, and went away. But if I had kept on ten minutes more, I could have laid that building flat in the street. And, with the same vibrator, I could drop the Brooklyn Bridge into the East River in less than an hour." He told the reporter he could also split the entire planet Earth in two the same way. "It might take more than a year to succeed, but in a few weeks, I could set the earth's crust into such a state of vibration that it would rise and fall hundreds of feet, throwing rivers out of their beds, wrecking buildings, and practically destroying civilization. The principle cannot fail."

While experimenting with the transmission of wireless power, Tesla developed a remote-controlled boat he called a teleautomaton. This single invention laid the foundation for devices we take for granted today, including garage door openers, fax machines, and remote controls for televisions, stereos, and toy cars. Tesla introduced the teleautomaton to the Institute of Electrical Engineers in May 1898 at the Electrical Exposition in Madison Square Garden in New York City. Because the Spanish-American War was being fought in Cuba at the same time, the primary theme of the exposition had become ways to defeat the Spanish.

Tesla demonstrated his teleautomaton, which was four feet long and three feet high, in a large tank in the center of an auditorium. With remote control transmitters, Tesla stood outside the tank and started and stopped the boat, steered it in various directions, and turned its lights on and off. Tesla then attempted to entertain his audience, which ultimately may have detracted from the complexity and importance of his invention. He challenged the audience to ask the teleautomaton questions and told them it would answer them by blinking its lights—once for yes, twice for no. The audience was

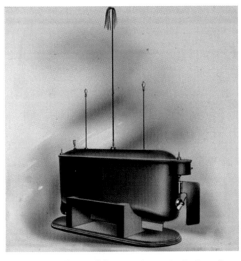

Tesla's submergible remote-controlled craft.

amazed. Tesla even had to open it up to prove that there was no one hiding inside.

Tesla's larger vision for his invention was to revolutionize how wars were fought. He believed that remote-controlled machines could eventually fight wars with no loss of life. He proposed remote-controlled torpedoes discharged from submarines: "My submarine boat, loaded with its torpedoes, can start out from a protected bay or be dropped over a ship side, make its devious way along the surface, through dangerous channels of mine beds . . . watching for its prey, then dart upon it at a favorite moment . . . discharge its deadly weapon and return to the hand that sent it. . . . I am aware that this sounds almost incredible and I have refrained from making this invention public until I had worked out practically every detail." While these ideas might not sound far-fetched to us, in Tesla's time they were extraordinary.

REMOTE CONTROLS

Remote controls are a major part of our everyday lives. They allow us to do all sorts of tasks more conveniently and easily—from unlocking car doors at the push of a button, to changing the channel on the television without getting up, to manipulating vehicles and robots in outer space. In order to ensure that when you change the channel your neighbor's television does not change, remote controls are tuned to work on different frequencies. Just as radio stations are broadcast at different frequencies so you can hear the station of your choice, so are remote controls segregated on the airwaves.

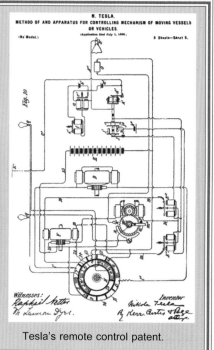

Tesla's remote control patent.

Knowing that his invention was likely to be mocked by those who did not understand it, Tesla did not allow newspaper reporters to witness his teleautomaton. The big news from the exposition, then, was Marconi's latest invention: a wireless detonation system that used a remote control much less sophisticated and developed than Tesla's. Thomas Edison's son, Tom Jr., was appointed to assist in the demonstrations. Marconi placed "bombs" on model Spanish ships, Tom Junior pushed a button, and the ships exploded. Unlike Tesla, Marconi had not yet discovered how to tune the frequencies of the remote control transmitters, and Tom Jr. inadvertently blew up a desk in the back room that contained other "bombs."

Though Marconi's invention was less sophisticated than Tesla's, his willingness to showcase it earned him more publicity. Many reporters who praised Marconi turned on Tesla, ridiculing him and sneering at his wild ideas and strange mannerisms. Even Tesla's old friend T. C. Martin published a critical editorial in *Electrical Engineer:* "Mr. Tesla fools himself, if he fools anybody, when he launches into the dazzling theories and speculations associated with his name."

Tesla could shrug off the rest of the criticism, but Martin's attack wounded him deeply. Tesla wrote a letter of complaint to Martin at the *Electrical Engineer,* saying that his honor had been offended and he would only forgive his longtime friend if he would apologize. Martin did not, and his friendship with Tesla was over.

The truth was nobody in Tesla's time could comprehend the significance of his visions, so they reacted with derision. Tesla was further insulted when, in November 1898, the examiner in chief of patents insisted on coming to see Tesla's teleautomaton for himself before granting a patent. Tesla recalled, "I remember that when later I called on an official in Washington, with a view of offering the invention to the Government, he burst out in laughter. . . . Nobody thought then that there was the faintest prospect of perfecting such a device."

Despite the criticism of his teleautomaton, Tesla continued to seek investors. He approached John Jacob Astor III, a thirty-two-year-old financier with assets of nearly $100 million. Astor was something of an inventor himself, having patented a bicycle brake, a storage battery, an internal-combustion engine, a "flying machine," and a pneumatic walkway that won a prize at the 1893 Chicago World's Fair.

Astor and his wife, Ava, were also frequent visitors at the Johnsons. Astor fought in the Spanish-American War and returned to America a hero in August 1898. Tesla went to him in November of that year to ask his friend for financial and moral support. He told Astor of his vision of a wireless communication system. Such a system, he said, would mean that messages could be relayed across the ocean. News, music, stock market reports, secure military communications, and even pictures could be transmitted to any part of the world.

Astor was intrigued. On January 10, 1899, he and Tesla signed a contract whereby Astor would give Tesla $100,000. In return, Tesla gave Astor five hundred shares of stock in the Tesla Electric Company and made Astor chairman of the board of directors.

Around the same time, Tesla achieved another goal. Tesla was very class conscious and aspired to live among the elite of New York. He moved into the Waldorf-Astoria Hotel, the residence of some of the wealthiest and most prominent people of the day. The hotel had been built in two stages: the Waldorf by William Waldorf Astor in 1893 and the Astoria by his cousin John Jacob Astor in 1897. The Waldorf-Astoria quickly became the symbol of elegance and exclusivity, allowing only a select few to live there. The manager, George C. Boldt Sr., was an immigrant from eastern Europe who loved to surround himself with the latest inventions, including control panels on the elevators and electric buzzers. Boldt's wife designed the décor and furnished the hotel with exquisite furniture, flowers, and fragrances. Tesla felt safe and secure in the luxurious (and clean) environment.

Astor told Tesla he was interested in seeing improvements made for the fluorescent lamp. Fluorescent light is most often produced in a long tube that contains a vapor, usually mercury, under low pressure. When an electric current is passed through the vapor, ultraviolet radiation is produced that is converted into visible light by an internal coating on the tube. Tesla agreed to work on the fluorescent lamp, but, without Astor's knowledge, put that project aside temporarily in favor of his dream of the wireless transmission of power.

With Astor's backing and the necessary patents secured, Tesla now had the means to build his new experimental transmission station. He scouted around the country for suitable sites. He wrote to Leonard E. Curtis, his longtime friend and Westinghouse patent attorney: "My coils are producing 4,000,000 volts—sparks jumping from wall to ceilings are a fire hazard. This is a secret test. I must have electrical power, water, and my own laboratory. I will need a good carpenter who will follow instructions. . . . My work will be done late at night when the power load will be least."

Curtis, who lived in Colorado, did some research and wrote back, "All things arranged, land will be free. You will live at the Alta Vista Hotel. I have [financial] interest in the City Power Plant so electricity is free to you."

Tesla was elated. He would have everything he needed in Colorado Springs, plus a bonus: Colorado had fantastic lightning storms, which Tesla wanted to experience and study. Each flash of lightning produces several hundred million volts of electricity—much more than Tesla had ever produced in his laboratory. He was elated at the prospect of viewing such a phenomenal display of nature's power.

The remoteness of Colorado would also afford him more privacy in which to experiment with his most exciting and promising venture yet. New York, he worried, held too many spies who might steal his ideas.

He shipped his equipment to Colorado in the spring of 1899 and arrived there himself on May 18. He was greeted by Curtis, a few town officials, several society people, and the governor. Tesla's name was well known in the region as his alternating-current power transmission system was being used at several gold, silver, and lead mines in the area. He was escorted to the Alta Vista

The beautiful and remote town of Colorado Springs, Colorado. *(Library of Congress)*

Hotel, where he asked to live in room 207 because 207 is evenly divisible by three. He instructed the maid to deliver eighteen clean towels to his room every day.

Tesla hired a local carpenter, Joseph Dozier, who began construction on the experimental station on East Pike's Peak Avenue. The station, sixty feet wide and eighteen feet high, resembled a barn. An adjustable aerial on the roof could extend to two hundred feet, and was topped by a large copper ball three feet in diameter. As soon as construction on the laboratory began, Tesla had a tall fence erected around the property, complete with signs that said, "KEEP OUT—GREAT DANGER."

Inside the experimental station was a high-frequency generator and a Tesla coil forty-five feet in diameter. Tesla carefully wrote all his theories, equations, experiments, and annotations in a notebook. He also photographed many of his experiments. He would soon be ready to begin attempts at worldwide wireless transmission.

On July 3, 1899, Tesla was delighted to witness a spectacular electrical storm. The following day he recorded in his notebook, "Observations made last night. They were not to be easily forgotten for more than one reason. First of all a magnificent sight was afforded by the extraordinary display of lightning, no less than 10,000–12,000 discharges being witnessed inside of two hours. . . . Some . . . were of a wonderful brilliancy and showed often 10 or twice as many branches."

Inspired, Tesla began constructing what he dubbed a "magnifying transmitter," which he later pronounced to be his most important invention. The device was capable of producing lightning as powerful as that in nature. He literally electrified the ground for miles around. People some distance away reported seeing sparks arc between their heels and the ground when they walked. Horses received electric shocks through their hooves and began to stampede in the pastures surrounding the laboratory. Tesla and his assistants wore thick cork or rubber soles on their shoes so they would not get shocked. The noise produced by the lightning in the lab was so loud that Tesla and his assistants stuffed their ears with cotton. Nevertheless, their ears often hurt for hours after the end of an experiment.

One night in midsummer, Tesla put his tower to the ultimate test. He told his assistant, Kolman Czito, to close the switch, completing the electric circuit, when he gave the signal. He further instructed Czito not to open the switch until he received Tesla's command to do so.

Tesla stepped outside the laboratory. "Now!" he yelled to Czito, who obediently threw the switch and turned on the equipment. The ground began to vibrate as the electric current surged through the gigantic coil and up into the aerial. Then, astonishingly, lightning bolts over one hundred feet long crackled and shot out from the copper ball on top of the mast. The noise they created was deafening, heard twenty miles away in the town of Cripple Creek. Tesla stood still, gazing in rapture.

Suddenly all was quiet. Tesla called to Czito, who reported that the switch was still closed. Tesla believed

This photo of Tesla working in the Colorado Springs lab was taken as a publicity shot. *(Tesla Museum Archives)*

that the electric company had cut the power to his laboratory. Actually, Tesla's experiment had overloaded the electric company's generator and set it on fire, cutting off power to the entire town of Colorado Springs. As soon as the fire was extinguished, a backup generator was put in place. Tesla's power, meanwhile, was cut off. He begged to have it reinstated so he could continue his experiments, but he was refused. Tesla then offered to send a team to fix the main generator at his own expense. The power company officials agreed, and when the main generator was back online, Tesla could resume his experiments.

Late one night the equipment began receiving a distinct pattern of sounds: blip . . . blip blip . . . blip blip blip. Tesla was elated; he was certain that he had just received communication from another planet—most likely Mars, he thought. He further postulated that the beings that sent the signals were of superior intelligence and scientifically more advanced than humans.

Tesla published his Martian theory in a number of articles. "Martian fever" was rampant in America at that time. The public was obsessed with the idea that life existed on Earth's closest neighbor. Tesla's claim to have received a signal from Mars fueled the public's imagination. To some, Tesla was again elevated to the status of a hero as the first human to receive communication from Mars. Skeptics among his peers, however, branded him a crackpot, and the press had a field day quoting their derisive remarks.

Tesla's equipment undoubtedly did receive signals from space—though probably not from Mars, but rather from the stars via electromagnetic radiation. The universe emits wavelengths of energy which we call static when we hear it between radio stations on the dial. Tesla may have been the first person to receive and listen to radio waves from outer space.

While Tesla was in Colorado, his faithful assistant, George Scherff, stayed behind in New York to oversee Tesla's interests there and to keep him abreast of the latest news. One bit of news did not make Tesla happy: Marconi had succeeded in transmitting a wireless signal across the English Channel and was now working to transmit signals hundreds of miles across Europe. The public and the press were still enamored of the Italian. Tesla wrote to Scherff on September 22, 1899, "Do not worry about me. I am about a century ahead of the other fellows." He was right; many of his ideas were simply too fantastic for the skeptical public of his day.

NINE:
WARDENCLYFFE

Tesla returned to New York in a new century, on January 8, 1900, with big plans. His Colorado experiments had exceeded his expectations, and he was now ready to construct a wireless transmitter that he believed would furnish power to the entire planet. Meanwhile, the press continued to publish articles mocking his belief that superior life existed on Mars.

Even though Tesla's Martian theory had made him the object of ridicule among some of his peers, many still believed in his inventions. Tesla convinced his friend Robert Johnson, now the editor of *Century*, to publish an article that he would write explaining his vision for worldwide communication. Marconi was thus far transmitting signals only from one specific point to another. Tesla's plan would utilize the Earth's ionosphere to transmit communication around the globe.

Stanford White, a renowned architect, read the article and asked Tesla to meet with him. He sat enthralled as Tesla outlined his plan for worldwide communication. White insisted on being part of the project, and began designing the building that would house the worldwide transmitter.

Tesla continued to court the wealthy, hoping that someone would give him the money he needed to construct his worldwide transmitter. He became frustrated when no one stepped forward, and was even more frustrated to read in the newspapers of Marconi's rising fame. The final blow came when Tesla learned that Edison, Marconi, and his former friend Michael Pupin had formed a partnership to produce radios. Tesla was convinced that Marconi had infringed on his patents and was being publicly credited for them

Salvation finally came from J. Pierpont Morgan, who had been intrigued by Tesla's article in *Century* magazine and wanted to hear more. Tesla explained that if he invested in his worldwide communication system, Morgan would have control of worldwide broadcasting.

But what Tesla did not tell Morgan was that his real goal was to transmit not wireless communication but wireless *power* around the globe. If Morgan knew of Tesla's true intentions, he most likely would have refused to invest, because a device to wirelessly transmit power would render obsolete other devices Morgan had invested in.

Morgan agreed to loan Tesla $150,000. Tesla promised Morgan that he would make his initial investment "worth 100 times the sum you have put at my disposal in such a magnanimous, princely way." Morgan insisted that Tesla sign over

J. P. Morgan. *(Library of Congress)*

fifty-one percent interest in his radio patents as collateral for the loan.

Now all Tesla needed was land on which to build. Stanford White had already designed a tower that was 187 feet high, with a steel shaft inside it that went down 120 feet into the ground. Tesla acquired two hundred acres of land at Shoreham on Long Island, New York, from James D. Warden. In gratitude, Tesla named the place Wardenclyffe. He assembled a team, and construction of the tower began.

On December 12, 1901, Tesla heard the bitter news that Marconi had just wirelessly transmitted the letter *S* across the Atlantic Ocean, from Cornwall, England, to Newfoundland, Canada. Marconi had used no less than seventeen of Tesla's patents to accomplish this feat.

This illustration touts Tesla's vision of the wireless tower at Wardenclyffe and served to promote what Tesla called his "World System," an amazingly accurate prophecy of the electronic capabilities we have today. *(Tesla Museum Archives)*

Nevertheless, Marconi was hailed as a hero and given credit for the invention of radio. When Tesla was asked to comment on Marconi's accomplishment, he replied, "Marconi is a donkey."

Tesla's funds were dwindling fast, and he appealed to

Morgan for more. But Morgan was losing interest in Tesla's plans for Wardenclyffe. Marconi had just accomplished what Tesla planned to do—transmitting wireless communication—without the expense of building anything like Wardenclyffe. Morgan refused to give Tesla any more money.

Tesla decided it was time to tell Morgan of his *real* goal—the wireless transmission of power, not just communication. On July 3, 1903, Tesla wrote to the financier, explaining the concept, and saying, "If I would have told you such as this before, you would have fired me out of your office. . . . Will you help me or let my great work— almost complete—go to pots?"

Morgan would not be swayed. On July 14, Tesla read his response: "I have received your letter . . . and in reply would say that I should not feel disposed at present to make any further advances."

Tesla began to lay off his crew. Even the faithful George Scherff had to take a second job as a bookkeeper for other companies. Tesla continued to bombard Morgan with requests for capital. At first his letters to Morgan were pleas, but as Morgan continued to ignore him, the letters became bitter and angry. Other investors heard of Tesla's plight and Morgan's refusal to lend him more capital. They trusted Morgan's judgment and began to think that Wardenclyffe was an unattainable dream. Tesla's entreaties to bankers and others were fruitless.

The situation was becoming desperate. Bill collectors were hounding Tesla. The electric company at Colorado Springs began billing him for the electricity he had used—despite the fact Leonard Curtis had assured Tesla the electricity was free. The city of Colorado Springs began billing him for the water he had used as well. In a letter to the city council, Tesla replied that the people of Colorado Springs should have felt honored that a great scientist such as he had chosen their town to erect his experimental station, and should therefore be happy to donate the water. Unfortunately, the city council did not agree.

Wardenclyffe, though not ready to transmit power worldwide, had begun to produce small coils to be used in the medical industry that earned some profit. Tesla also had plans for a new turbine that he was sure would restore him to fortune and fame.

The following year, 1904, brought another stunning blow: Marconi was finally granted a patent for the invention of radio. Tesla sued but did not have the financial resources to see the suit through.

It is easy to think that Marconi's successful patent application marked the beginning of the end for Nikola Tesla. But while Marconi's victory was a major setback, it is hard to separate its effect from the damage done by years of radiation to which Tesla had exposed himself, or the increasing demands his obsessive disorders put on his aging body. Whatever the cause, Tesla began a descent from which he would not recover.

Soon after Marconi received his patent, many of

Tesla's began to expire. This meant that anyone could use his ideas without paying him royalties. There were also several serious accidents at Wardenclyffe. No lives were lost, but Scherff was badly burned when hot molten lead exploded in his face. Doctors thought for a time that he would lose his sight.

Then George Westinghouse turned his back on his old friend. Tesla had been getting machinery for Wardenclyffe from the Westinghouse corporation, and he wrote to ask for capital, promising that Westinghouse would soon benefit from Tesla's greatest invention yet: "Has anything happened to mar the cordiality of our relations? I would be very sorry, not only because of my admiration for you but for other serious reasons. The transmission of power without wires will very soon create an industrial revolution and such as the world has never seen before. Who is to be more helpful in this great development, and who will derive from it greater benefits than yourself?" Westinghouse declined to help.

Tesla's emotional state continued to decline. As is common in someone who is suffering an emotional collapse, his handwriting began to deteriorate until it became illegible. George Scherff resigned from the Wardenclyffe project in the fall of 1906. This blow further depressed Tesla. He scrawled a letter to Katharine Johnson, saying, "I'm ever in so much greater trouble." In a heroic gesture, Katharine hired a hansom cab and ordered the driver to take her to J. Pierpont Morgan's office. She intended to appeal to him on her friend's

The elegant Waldorf-Astoria Hotel at the turn of the century.

behalf. When she arrived, Morgan refused to see her.

Despite pleas from the Johnsons and others to join them at dinners, the theater, and other activities, Tesla withdrew from society. He would not allow sunlight into his hotel room at the Waldorf-Astoria. His only company was the pigeons he fed on his windowsill. Every so often he would allow the pigeons to come into his room. Tesla had long had an affinity for these birds and fed them regularly on the sidewalks and parks of New York City.

Tesla shunned doctors and was determined to cure himself. As part of his self-prescribed therapy, he would take a midnight train to Long Island. There, at Wardenclyffe, he attached wires to his skull and allowed high-frequency electricity to flow through his brain. He claimed that this kept him alive.

Tesla was momentarily bolstered by his induction into the New York Academy of Sciences in May 1907. He had begun to think that his dream of supplying the world with unlimited wireless power might be too far ahead of its time, so he began concentrating on "other inventions which appealed more to practical men." He believed that what the world needed was a "prime mover," which he intended to provide in the form of the bladeless turbine he had begun to develop four years earlier. Turbines up

Tesla's 10,000-horsepower, bladeless steam turbine was looked upon with great skepticism by his contemporaries. *(Tesla Museum Archives)*

to this time had blades like a propeller that were slowed down by the viscosity, or thickness, of the medium in which they turned. On Tesla's bladeless turbine, disks would replace the blades and would actually speed up with increasing viscosity. Thus the problem that friction created by slowing down the spin of the blades would be eliminated.

Tesla envisioned a revolution in power transmission. His turbine could be fueled by gasoline, water, steam, or wind, and could power cars, airplanes, ocean liners, trains, and trucks. It could be used in many industries, including irrigation, mining, and agriculture. He was encouraged when the concept of his bladeless turbine received wide acclaim. Even the War Department of the United States was impressed, and declared it to be "something new in the world." Tesla began to hope that his days of poverty were over.

In reality, like wireless power, the concept of the bladeless turbine was ahead of its time. Tesla had many problems with prototypes, as the best materials for producing such a turbine had not yet been developed. It was not until the latter half of the twentieth century— after his death—that Tesla's concept was perfected and his bladeless turbine was afforded its due recognition. Once again, Tesla's hopes for changing the world were dashed and his name was associated with wild ideas of little practical value. History, he could only hope, would be kinder.

TEN: SETBACKS

Lacking a steady source of income, Nikola Tesla was generally broke. What little money he had went to bird-seed for his beloved pigeons, and then to the salaries of his employees. Despite his eccentricities, Tesla's staff and friends were loyal to him. The manager of the Waldorf-Astoria Hotel, George Boldt, had overlooked Tesla's nonpayment of rent for three years. But now he was becoming impatient. Boldt had become a million-aire and had created the Lincoln Trust Company, a bank located across from the hotel. Rather than evict the scientist, Boldt agreed to accept the deeds on Wardenclyffe as payment. Tesla gave them over, believing that his fortunes would turn, investors would appear, and he would get Wardenclyffe in full operation. Then he would be able to buy back the deeds from Boldt.

HOTEL NEW YORKER

March 2, 1942

Carl:

I have thought that the total quantity of vegetables might be increased to 112 ounces. Furthermore, I have, eliminated all doubtful items. On this supposition I give the relative weights of the components and their protein values on the next page.

Total amount of vegetables		N × 6.25
112 ounces		
Leeks (only the white)	2 ounces	0.80
Heart of cabbage	24 "	2.80
Carrots	8 "	0.60
Cauliflower (only the flower)	12 "	1.80
Celery heart	8 "	0.65
White potato	8 "	1.00
Sweet potato	12 "	1.50
Spinach	12 "	1.73
Fresh tomato	8 "	0.60
White turnip	10 "	0.82
Lettuce heart	4 "	0.30
Tapioca	4 "	0.52

Total weight of vegetables 112 " Protein total 13.12 equal to about 13 grams

Tesla's intricate recipe for pigeon food.

But the American economy began to decline in August 1907. No one wanted to invest in Wardenclyffe or anything else. Banks began to fail as panicked customers drew out all their money. J. Pierpont Morgan called an emergency meeting of bank and trust presidents. He proposed buying out all the failing financial institutions that looked like they could be saved. The presidents hesitated, however, and thus many smaller banks went broke.

Tesla's failures and disappointments began to prey on him. He began to write angry and sometimes rambling letters to magazines and newspapers. He reviewed for the readers how he had invented the technology that others pirated. He outlined clearly how he, not Marconi, had developed radio. He reminded the public that he had invented the alternating-current polyphase system, the fluorescent light, the induction motor, various mechani-

cal and electrical oscillators, remote control, and wireless transmission of power and communication. Finally,
lest the public forget, he was the first to receive a
communication from Mars. Some of these letters were
published, others were filed away and forgotten.

Tesla's inventive mind continued to produce. He
began work on a flying machine, which he called a
"flivver plane." The Wright brothers, Wilbur and Orville,
had by this time flown their airplane many times. Tesla's,
however, was different. It was to be powered by his

A drawing from Tesla's patent for his "flivver plane."

bladeless turbine and would resemble a flying stove. It would weigh only eight hundred pounds, take off vertically, and could fly in and out of windows if necessary. He was honored in early 1908 at a dinner at the Waldorf-Astoria, and in his speech explained his vision of air travel. "My airship will have neither gas bag [as a blimp or hot air balloon], wings nor propellers . . . You might see it on the ground and you would never guess that it was a flying machine. Yet it will be able to move at will through the air in any direction with perfect safety, higher speeds than have yet been reached, regardless of weather . . . or downward currents. It can remain absolutely stationary in the air even in a wind for a great length of time."

Tesla never built a prototype of his flivver plane, but in the latter part of the twentieth century such aircraft were designed and built by the military. One such example is the Marine Corps' V-22 Osprey that can take off like a helicopter and fly like an airplane.

Tesla continued to invent and received patents on many kinds of electronic devices, but he never gave up on his plans for Wardenclyffe. In the end, money was his downfall. First, he was sued for nonpayment of his mortgages; then, in a particularly painful blow, the Westinghouse corporation sued Tesla for equipment he received but did not pay for. Westinghouse was awarded a judgment against Tesla of $23,500. Tesla had no money, so Westinghouse went to Wardenclyffe and salvaged what equipment was left.

J. Pierpont Morgan died in April 1913. A month after the funeral, Tesla approached J. P. Morgan Jr. to discuss the continuation of funding that his father had begun. The younger Morgan was impressed with Tesla's bladeless turbine and agreed to loan him $15,000 at six percent interest for nine months. Tesla reminded him that his father had invested $150,000 in Wardenclyffe. Morgan responded by asking Tesla to begin repaying the $150,000.

Morgan then went on an extended European vacation, and when he returned in December 1913, Tesla again appealed to him for money. "I am almost despairing at the present state of things. I need money badly and cannot get it in these dreadful times. You are about the only man to whom I can look for help." In reply, Morgan sent Tesla a bill for $684.17, interest owed on two loans, and wished him a Merry Christmas.

Tesla continued to appeal to Morgan over the next few years, but Morgan was not particularly interested in wireless transmission and advanced Tesla only another $10,000.

Never good with money, Tesla's finances were now totally out of his control. He had run up a bill of $20,000 at the Waldorf-Astoria. In 1915, Boldt informed Tesla that because of his unpaid rent, Boldt now owned Wardenclyffe. Tesla was in shock. When he deeded Wardenclyffe to Boldt, he never expected him to collect on the deal.

Wardenclyffe now belonged to Boldt, but he had no idea what to do with the remnants of the center for worldwide wireless transmission. After Tesla's crew had vacated the premises, vandals had broken in and destroyed what was left. Tesla's papers and notes were strewn about and equipment was smashed. Boldt approached the United States War Department to ask if they were interested in using it for security purposes. The beginning of the first World War had raised concerns about the safety of the coastline. The War Department declined. The site was even considered for a pickle factory, but nothing came of that either.

Soon after Tesla lost Wardenclyffe, a strange incident occurred. In 1909, Tesla's rival Marconi had been awarded the Nobel Prize in Physics for his development of wireless communication, unashamedly using Tesla's patents illegally and claiming the work as his own. From that point on, as far as the world was concerned, it was Marconi who invented radio. But in November of 1915, the *New York Times* reported that Tesla and Edison were

The tower and power plant at Wardenclyffe in Shoreham, Long Island. *(Tesla Museum Archives)*

to share the Nobel Prize in Physics. In an interview with the *Times* on November 7, Tesla said that he had not been informed of the award, but he believed he was being honored because of his work in wireless transmission. Tesla had hopes the Nobel committee would set the record straight about the true origins of radio. Excitedly, he told the newspaper that one day, not only voices but even pictures would be transmitted around the world instantaneously. The reading public was incredulous; they could not imagine such a thing. Still, newspapers and magazines across the country reported the story of Tesla and Edison's impending award. Nikola Tesla was a headline name once again.

One week later, Tesla and the rest of the world were stunned when British scientists Sir William Henry Bragg and his son William Lawrence Bragg were awarded the Nobel Prize in Physics for their use of x-rays in the analysis of the structure of crystals. The Nobel Committee had no comment on the reports that Edison and Tesla were to have been the recipients. A rumor immediately began to circulate that Tesla had refused to share the award with Edison, so the committee gave it to the Braggs, but this was never substantiated. To this day, no really knows the truth about the incident. What is certain is that Tesla could have used the $20,000 prize.

In March of 1916, Tesla was summoned to court for failing to pay the city of New York $935 in personal taxes. Marconi, Edison, Westinghouse, and others were making millions from his patents while he was penniless.

His plight was brought to the attention of Bernard A. Behrend, a Swiss engineer who had recently immigrated to the United States. Behrend had long admired Tesla and was appalled to learn of his poverty. In 1917, he nominated Tesla for the Edison Medal, a prestigious award previously won by Westinghouse, Alexander Graham Bell, and Elihu Thomson. At first, Behrend's plan backfired when Tesla was offended by the nomination and refused to receive it. He still harbored bitter feelings toward Edison, whom he felt was honored each time the medal bearing his name was awarded. Behrend, however, talked Tesla into accepting the award by asking him if he wanted to be remembered as the inventor of his alternating-current power system, or if he would be content to allow imposters to continue to claim the credit.

The presentation of the Edison Medal was to be made on May 18, 1917, at the Engineers Club, following a sumptuous banquet. Robert and Katharine Johnson were among Tesla's loyal fans who attended the ceremony. Tesla was dressed in his finest tuxedo and tails.

As the banquet ended and the presentation of the medal was about to begin, Behrend noticed in horror that Tesla was missing. He enlisted the aid of the staff, who searched the building, looking into restrooms and closets. Behrend himself rushed outside, thinking that Tesla may have had a last-minute change of heart about receiving the Edison Medal. On a hunch he hurried to Bryant Park, one of Tesla's favorite places to walk, think, and feed the pigeons.

Bryant Park and the New York Public Library, where Tesla often liked to sit and feed the pigeons. *(Library of Congress)*

Sure enough, Behrend found Tesla in the park—standing stock-still and covered from head to toe with pigeons. As Behrend approached, Tesla put a finger to his mouth to caution him to be quiet. The pigeons were eating seed from his hands and even pecking seed that he had placed on his lips. Finally, Tesla gently shook the pigeons off and accompanied Behrend to the presentation.

Behrend's introduction of his friend and mentor was eloquent: "Were we to seize and eliminate from our industrial world the results of Mr. Tesla's work, the wheels of industry would cease to turn, our electric cars and trains would stop, our towns would be dark, our mills would be dead and idle. Yes, so far reaching is his work that it has become the warp and woof of industry. . . . His

THOMAS A · EDISON *and the* EDISON MEDALISTS

This poster commemorates fourteen recipients of the Edison Medal, including Tesla.

name marks an epoch in the advance of electrical science. From that work has sprung a revolution."

While being awarded the Edison Medal was an honor, it could in no way compensate for what was to happen two months later. The United States had entered World War I in April 1917. German U-boats (submarines) were sinking the ships of America and her allies, and rumors spread that the Germans were occupying Wardenclyffe, using it as a base for espionage.

On July 4, 1917, a charge of dynamite was detonated inside the Wardenclyffe tower in an attempt to destroy it. It was so solidly built, however, that it took many charges of dynamite to complete the job. People said that the government had blown it up, but the truth is that the management of the Waldorf-Astoria had hired the Smiley Steel Company to destroy Wardenclyffe. The management intended to sell off any salvageable parts to cover Tesla's unpaid rent to the hotel. After paying off Smiley Steel, the hotel netted only $1,750, hardly enough to cover Tesla's debts.

Tesla was bitter and broke. He packed his belongings

The Wardenclyffe tower leans precariously to the side after it was dynamited on July 4, 1917. *(Tesla Wardenclyffe Project Archives)*

and, after twenty years, left the Waldorf-Astoria Hotel and moved into the Hotel St. Regis. For the next nine years, he spent most of his time in Chicago, Boston, Philadelphia, and Milwaukee working as an engineering consultant for large companies such as Allis-Chalmers and the Waltham Watch Company. He continued to invent as well, and produced a speedometer, a tacho-meter, and a motor used in motion-picture equipment. Tesla coils were being put to good use in that industry as well, since they could provide lightning on demand. He also spent a great deal of time trying to perfect his bladeless turbine.

Robert and Katharine Johnson moved to Italy in 1920, when Robert was appointed ambassador to that country. Many of Tesla's other friends had already died, including Mark Twain in 1910. Left alone most of the time, Tesla's eccentricities became more pronounced. He walked around the block of the St. Regis Hotel three times before he went inside. He avoided stepping on cracks in the sidewalk and became even more fanatical about germs and hand washing. He spent a lot of time walking the streets of New York at night, feeding the pigeons. He explained to the *Electrical World* magazine, "Sometimes I feel that by not marrying I made too great a sacrifice to my work, so I have decided to lavish all the affection of a man no longer young on the feathery tribe. . . . To care for those homeless, hungry or sick birds is the delight of my life. It is my only means of playing."

Tesla lavished his affection on one pigeon in particular. He felt a strong connection to the bird and rendered speechless two reporters when he told them this story: "I have been feeding pigeons, thousands of them, for years. . . . But there was one pigeon, a beautiful

Tesla's beloved pigeon. *(Tesla Museum Archives)*

bird, pure white with light gray tips on its wings; that one was different. It was a female. I would know that pigeon anywhere. No matter where I was that pigeon would find me; when I wanted her I had only to wish and call her and she would come flying to me. She understood me and I understood her. I loved that pigeon. Yes, I loved her as a man loves a woman, and she loved me. When she was ill I knew, and understood; she came to my room and I stayed beside her for days. I nursed her back to health. That pigeon was the joy of my life. If she needed me, nothing else mattered. As long as I had her, there was a purpose in my life.

"Then one night as I was lying in my bed in the dark, solving problems, as usual, she flew in through the open window and stood on my desk. I knew she wanted me; she wanted to tell me something important so I got up and went to her. As I looked at her I knew she wanted to tell me she was dying. And then, as I got her message, there came a light from her eyes—powerful beams of light.

"Yes, it was real light, a powerful, dazzling, blinding light, a light more intense than I had ever produced by the most powerful lamps in my laboratory. When that pigeon died, something went out of my life. Up to that time I knew with a certainty that I would complete my work, no matter how ambitious my program, but when that something went out of my life I knew my life's work was finished. Yes, I have fed pigeons for years; I continue to feed them, thousands of them, for after all, who can tell—."

The reporters who heard this story were dumbfounded. In the years since it was initially reported, psychologists have tried to understand what Tesla's obsession with animals, and one pigeon in particular, meant. Others have chosen to see his feelings for this pigeon as just another symptom of his unusual personality. The management of the hotels Tesla lived in took a very practical view: Tesla allowed his pigeon friends into his rooms where they proceeded to scatter seeds and droppings. This was unacceptable and, genius or not, Tesla was evicted from several hotels. His faithful pigeons, undaunted, followed him from one window ledge to another.

ELEVEN:
THE DEATH RAY

Tesla's great years as a scientist were mostly behind him. Though he would continue to think, speculate, and sketch ideas until his death, as he aged Tesla gave himself over to increasingly odd or misguided ideas. He remained a hero to the next generation of scientists, however, who flocked to Tesla in hopes of soaking up some of his inventiveness and ingenuity. They would also work together to help the older man when he, like millions of other Americans, was financially strapped during the Great Depression.

During the 1920s and 1930s, Tesla found occasional work as a consulting engineer, supplementing his meager income with money from friends and even a few dollars from admirers in Europe. During this time, he began work on what would be his last consuming pas-

Beginning: "My Inventions," by Nikola Tesla

FEB. 1919 20 CTS. **ELECTRICAL** OVER 100 ILLUST.

EXPERIMENTER

SCIENCE AND INVENTION

THE TESLA
WIRELESS LIGHT
SEE PAGE 692

Tesla and his work on wireless technology were featured in the February 1919 issue of *Electrical Experimenter*.

sion—and perhaps his most bizarre, since no one actually knows if it ever really existed.

Rumors had been circulating for years that Nikola Tesla had invented a weapon more powerful and destructive than any on earth. An article on the front page of the *New York Times* on July 11, 1934, read, "Tesla, at 78, Bares New 'Death Beam.'" The article continued to say that the weapon "will send concentrated beams of particles through the free air, of such tremendous energy that they will bring down a fleet of 10,000 enemy airplanes at a distance of 250 miles." Tesla said, "This new beam of mine consists of minute bullets [of energy] moving at a terrific speed, and any amount of power desired can be transmitted by them." He went on to say that he incorporated four entirely new inventions in his particle beam weapon, including a new process for producing massive electrical power and a method for amplifying it.

Tesla was working to perfect his invention in two secret laboratories—one under the Fifty-Ninth Street Bridge near Second Avenue—that were discovered only after his death. Though dubbed the "death ray," Tesla preferred to think of his invention as a "peace beam" and insisted that it would be used only for defensive purposes.

Tesla approached J. P. Morgan Jr. and tried to interest him in the machine. He needed money to build a prototype. Morgan was unconvinced that it was feasible and declined to help.

Tesla then tried to interest other nations in his weapon. He sent a highly technical paper, describing his invention, to the governments of the United States, England, Canada, France, the Soviet Union, and Yugoslavia. This prompted J. Edgar Hoover, head of the FBI at the time, to begin keeping a file on Tesla. Tesla also drew the FBI's attention because he had been speaking out against President Franklin Delano Roosevelt's "New Deal" plan for the United States, and because some of his associates were said to be Communists.

Tesla, now living at the Hotel Governor Clinton, was again behind in his rent. He offered to the hotel management a "working model" of his particle beam weapon in lieu of cash, saying that it was worth $10,000. The hotel accepted, and the device and a written receipt were placed in locker number 103 in the hotel's vault.

On July 10, 1931, Tesla turned seventy-five years old.

Tesla on the cover of *Time* at age seventy-five.

Time magazine honored him by putting his picture on the cover and printing an interview. In it, Tesla announced that he was researching "an entirely new and unsuspected source" of energy, but would not elaborate. He chose instead to surprise the interviewer by speaking eloquently of his plans for a device that would signal the stars. Tesla said, "I think that nothing can be more important than interplanetary communication. It will certainly come some day, and the certitude that there are other human beings in the universe, working, suffering, struggling like ourselves, will produce a magic effect on mankind, and will form the foundation of a universal brotherhood that will last as long as humanity itself."

Edison died three months later. Perhaps it was the death of his nemesis that brought him out of isolation, but Tesla began celebrating all his subsequent birthdays by inviting the press to his apartment and describing to them his latest ideas and inventions.

In 1935, another nemesis became gravely ill. Michael Pupin requested that Tesla be located and brought to his hospital room so that Pupin could make peace with him. Through the years, since his split with Tesla, Pupin had insisted that many of Tesla's inventions were his own. He particularly claimed the alternating-current polyphase system. As a professor at Columbia College, he never mentioned Tesla's name in his lectures. Now that he was dying, however, he felt guilty and wanted to make amends.

Pupin asked Stanko Stoilkovic, the Yugoslavian ambassador to America, for help. The first time Stoilkovic had met Tesla in 1918, Tesla had been standing in front of the New York library feeding pigeons from the palm of his hand. This time, Stoilkovic approached Tesla's door and found him wearing his favorite red robe and blue slippers. Tesla was surprised to hear of Pupin's deathbed request. He told Stoilkovic that he would have to sleep on it. He contacted Stoilkovic the next day and agreed to meet with Pupin as long as Stoilkovic accompanied him.

The meeting took place in Pupin's hospital room. Tesla approached the bed and said, "How are you, my old friend?" That was all he needed to say; Pupin cried from relief. They shared a few moments together, and Tesla left the room. As soon as Tesla left, Pupin passed away.

Tesla's old friend Robert Johnson was four years older than Tesla and in declining health. In 1937, Tesla gave Robert a copy of a new biography of himself that had been written in Serbo-Croatian and translated into English. Robert was touched, but far too weak to write a thank you letter, so had someone else do it for him. He signed it, though—"R. U. Johnson—Luka Filipov." Robert died later that year on October 14. Katharine had preceded him in death twelve years earlier.

Late one night, not long after Robert died, Tesla was hit by a taxi while feeding the pigeons near St. Patrick's Cathedral. True to form, he refused medical help and limped home. He had wrenched his back and cracked three ribs. For the next six months he was bedridden and fought off several bouts of pneumonia.

The executives of Westinghouse Electric felt guilty when they heard of Tesla's accident. George Westinghouse had died in 1914, but the current management knew that if it had not been for Tesla, Westinghouse Electric probably would not exist. In a gesture of rapprochement, they offered to pay his rent for the rest of his life.

Though many of Tesla's longtime friends had died, he was a hero to many of the younger generation. They looked after him. The science writer Kenneth Swezey was only nineteen when he first met Tesla, who he came to view as almost a god, and wrote many articles about him. In Tesla's last years, Swezey and the inventor were often together. Swezey even accompanied Tesla on his midnight outings to feed his beloved pigeons.

The other person closest to Tesla during his declining years was his nephew, Sava Kosanovic. He was also one reason the federal government took a strong interest in Tesla, because they suspected he was sympathetic to the Communist party. Kosanovic had been Yugoslavia's first

Eighty-six-year-old Tesla meets King Peter II of Yugoslavia on July 15, 1942. Tesla's nephew, Sava Kosanovic, holds his uncle's arm. *(Tesla Museum Archives)*

ambassador to America and was the chairman of the Yugoslav Economic Mission. He cared for Tesla as the great scientist aged, while simultaneously working to set up a museum in Belgrade to honor his uncle, who had become a national hero in his homeland.

Age was catching up with Tesla. He abandoned food and subsisted almost exclusively on a diet of warm milk. He became increasingly confused and distracted, but he would not give up on his final project. High-level government officials were intrigued by Tesla's work, and they scheduled a meeting at the White House for January 8, 1943.

Just after New Year's Day in 1943, Tesla sent for a messenger boy. He told the boy his friend Mark Twain was in financial trouble and gave him an envelope with some money to deliver to Twain at 35 South Fifth Avenue. The boy went out into a raging winter storm and tried to find the address. When he could not, he returned to Tesla's room. Tesla sent him out again, and this time also asked him to feed the pigeons. The boy consulted with his supervisor, who told him that Mark Twain had died twenty-five years earlier. Moreover, the address Tesla had given the messenger no longer existed. It was the address of Tesla's first laboratory, and South Fifth Avenue had long since become West Broadway. The messenger returned to Tesla, who grew angry and insisted that Mark Twain had visited him in his room just the night before.

A few days later, Tesla complained of chest pains.

Again he refused medical help and told the maid when she came to clean his room not to come back, and to put the *Do Not Disturb* sign on the door as she left. Two days later, the maid tiptoed into Tesla's room and found him dead. The coroner estimated the time of death as 10:30 PM on January 7, 1943. Nikola Tesla, eighty-six years old, had died peacefully in his sleep.

Swezey and Kosanovic were notified of Tesla's death and hurried to his apartment. Kosanovic was surprised to find his uncle's body had already been removed and taken to Campbell's Funeral Parlor at Madison Avenue and 81st Street. He was further upset when he realized that Tesla's belongings had been searched and that some of Tesla's technical papers were missing, as was a thick black notebook that Kosanovic knew his uncle kept. Kosanovic also knew that Tesla had labeled many of the missing papers "Government." This fueled his suspicions that the FBI had already been through the room.

Kosanovic was correct. Because of the sensitive nature of Tesla's work on his particle beam weapon, and because World War II was in full sway, the FBI had gone to Tesla's residence as soon as his death had been announced. When Kosanovic found this out, he accused the FBI of having stolen Tesla's papers. The FBI, however, denied that they removed anything. They accused Kosanovic of taking the papers and trying to use the FBI as a scapegoat. J. Edgar Hoover had placed Kosanovic under surveillance some time ago, believing that he sympathized with numerous communist and fascist Eu-

A document from Tesla's FBI file.

ropean government leaders. In a memo to his employees, Hoover said that he feared that, as heir to Tesla's estate, Kosanovic "might make certain material available to the enemy."

As the two sides fumed, Tesla's funeral was held on January 10 at the Cathedral of St. John the Divine in New York City. Two thousand people were in attendance, and the pallbearers were all Nobel Prize winners. Telegrams of condolence and praise poured in from all over the world. The mayor of New York City honored Tesla with an eloquent eulogy that was broadcast over the radio.

Just days later, the FBI turned the matter of Tesla's estate over to the Office of Alien Property (OAP). This was a curious move, since Tesla had been an American citizen for fifty years and no longer held alien (non-citizen) status. Nevertheless, the OAP went to the Hotel Governor Clinton to open locker 103 and retrieve the particle beam weapon. Inside the locker they found a receipt and a wooden box. Inside that box they found only a multi-decade resistance box, an instrument commonly used for measuring electrical resistance. The famous particle beam weapon was nowhere to be found.

The mystery remains unsolved to this day. Some people think the FBI had gotten to the locker before the OAP, removed the weapon, and substituted the resistance box for it. Others suspect that Tesla may never have actually built a working model of the particle beam weapon, and that he duped the Hotel Governor Clinton.

Following World War II, U.S. military intelligence obtained copies of Nikola Tesla's papers and sent them to Wright–Patterson Air Force Base in Dayton, Ohio, and a military operation, code-named "Project Nick," was undertaken to test the feasibility of Tesla's particle beam weapon. No results were ever published, and the copies of Tesla's papers disappeared. Nine years after Tesla's death, the OAP released some of Tesla's papers and other possessions to Kosanovic. He returned them to Belgrade, Yugoslavia, where a museum was finally created to honor Tesla.

For many years the Communist leader Josip Tito ruled Yugoslavia and forbade Western journalists from visiting the museum. However, personnel from the Soviet Union, another Communist country, were given free access to the museum and to all of Tesla's papers. In 1960, the Soviet leader Nikita Khrushchev caused worldwide concern when he announced that his country was developing a powerful new weapon. The United States government was even more concerned when, seventeen years later, in 1977, *Aviation Week* published an article about Soviet particle beam weapons. The article included detailed drawings of the Soviet weapon. The drawings bore an eerie resemblance to drawings Tesla had made of his "death ray."

For years, Tesla's papers on his so-called death ray were thought to be missing. It is now known that they are held in a classified library at a United States defense research agency, and are accessible only to members of the intelligence community. The reason why they have remained so closely guarded has never been revealed.

In 1943, the Marconi Wireless Telegraph Company of America sued the federal government for patent infringement in the U.S. Court of Claims. The government countersued, and the case went to the Supreme Court. In an attempt to settle the case, the Supreme Court not only examined all of Marconi's patents, it examined the patents of others who had invented electronic components similar to Marconi's. Among other things, the court found that Marconi, in his claim to have invented radio, had pirated several of Tesla's patents.

Only eight months after Tesla's death in 1943, the United States Supreme Court handed down a ruling of which few people are aware. The court declared Marconi's 1904 patent for radio invalid and awarded the patent to Tesla. Nevertheless, history books still credit Marconi with the invention of radio. Tesla is rarely even mentioned.

TIMELINE

1856 Born in Croatia.
1875 Enrolls in Polytechnic Institute in Graz, Austria.
1880 Enrolls in University of Prague.
1881 Suffers mental breakdown.
1882 Discovers rotating magnetic field.
1884 Emigrates to America; meets Edison; War of the Currents begins.
1885 Receives his first patent.
1888 Meets Westinghouse.
1891 Invents Tesla coil.
1893 First wireless transmission; Columbian Exposition; becomes American citizen.
1895 Lab burns to the ground.
1896 Harnesses the power of Niagara Falls to generate electricity.
1898 Moves into Waldorf-Astoria Hotel.
1899 Moves to Colorado Springs.
1900 Returns to New York.
1901 Signs contract with J. P. Morgan; construction on Wardenclyffe begins.
1906 Invents bladeless turbine.
1917 Wardenclyffe demolished; awarded Edison Medal.
1931 On cover of *Time* magazine for seventy-fifth birthday.
1943 Dies on January 8 in Hotel New Yorker; government seizes estate.

SOURCES

CHAPTER ONE: Croatia

p. 11-12, "the fountain of my . . . on a petal," Marc J. Seifert, *Wizard: The Life and Times of Nikola Tesla, Biography of a Genius* (New York: Citadel Press, 1996), 8.

p. 12, "They asked me . . ." Ibid., 10.

p. 14, "These creatures . . ." Nikola Tesla, *My Inventions* (Austin, TX: Hart Brothers, 1982), 45.

p. 14, "That disgusting sight . . ." Ibid.

p. 15, "I obtained tallow . . ." Ibid., 36.

p. 15-16, "Had I a sweet cake . . ." Nikola Tesla, "Some Personal Recollections," http://www.pbs.org/tesla/res/res_art01.html.

p. 16, "This change of residence . . ." Seifert, *Wizard,* 11.

CHAPTER TWO: New Horizons

p. 19, "One day I was handed . . ." Tesla, *My Inventions,* 53.

p. 20, "to [Twain's books] might have . . ." Ibid.

p. 21, "[A]nd so I began . . ." Ibid., 32.

p. 22, "It is impossible for me . . ." Ibid., 54.

p. 24, "Perhaps I may get well . . ." Ibid.

p. 25, "submarine tube . . . " Ibid., 55.

p. 25, "found just the right . . ." John J. O'Neill, *Prodigal Genius* (New York: Ives Washburn, 1944), 36.

p. 26, "was the most brilliant . . ." Tesla, *My Inventions,* 57.

p. 29, "The sooner you lose . . ." Ibid., 37.

p. 30, "tall and beautiful . . ." Seifert, *Wizard,* 18.

p. 32, "the body of Apollo . . ." Inez Hunt and Wanda Draper, *Lightning in His Hands: The Life Story of Nikola Tesla*

(Hawthorne, CA: Omni Publications, 1977), 33.

p. 33-34, "With me it was . . ." Tesla, *My Inventions,* 60-61.

p. 35, "The glow retreats . . ." Margaret Cheney, *Man Out of Time* (New York: Dell Publishing, 1981), 27.

p. 35-36, "In less than two months . . ." Tesla, *My Inventions,* 65.

CHAPTER THREE: Edison

p. 37, "the last twenty-nine days . . ." Ibid., 66.

p. 40, "the grass and the . . ." Cheney, *Man Out of Time,* 31.

p. 44, "I know two great men . . ." O'Neill, *Prodigal Genius,* 67.

p. 46, "That is a damn . . ." Ibid., 69.

p. 47, "Tesla, you don't understand . . ." Ibid., 70.

CHAPTER FOUR: The War of the Currents

p. 60, "It is hard to conceive . . ." Seifert, *Wizard,* 58.

p. 60, "to the horror of all present . . ." Ibid.

p. 60, "I have merely glanced . . ." Ibid.

CHAPTER FIVE: Going Wireless

p. 67, "While I was lecturing . . ." Dragislav Petkovich, "A Visit to Nikola Tesla," *Politika*, April 27, 1927, 3.

p. 70, "As I lay helpless there . . ." Tesla, *My Inventions,* 104.

p. 70, "a cloud carrying angelic . . ." Ibid.

CHAPTER SIX: Peculiarities

p. 77, "I have just seen . . ." Frederick Anderson, ed. *Mark Twain's Notebooks and Journals,* vol. 3, *1883-1891* (Berkeley, CA: University of California Press, 1979), 431.

p. 78, "I know I am completely . . ." W. T. Stephenson, "Electric Light of the Future," *Outlook*, March 9, 1895, 354-356.

p. 80, "I have never . . ." Seifert, *Wizard,* 124.

p. 82, "distinguished sweetness, sincerity . . ." Ibid., 130.

p. 82, "From under protruding eyebrows . . ." O'Neill, *Prodigal Genius,* 290-91.

p. 82-83, "I believe that a writer . . ." Cheney, *Man Out of Time,* 129.

p. 83, "the female mind . . ." O'Neill, *Prodigal Genius,* 306.

p. 86, "medieval practitioner . . ." Cheney, *Man Out of Time,* 97.

p. 86, "He required that . . ." O'Neill, *Prodigal Genius,* 292.

p. 86-87, "In Tesla's earlier years . . ." Ibid., 292-93.

CHAPTER SEVEN: Alternating Current

p. 90, "Two tottering brick walls . . ." T. C. Martin, "The Burning of Tesla's Laboratory," *Engineering Magazine,* April 1895, 101-104.

p. 92, "This long distance . . ." Seifert, *Wizard,* 149.

p. 92, "I am now convinced . . ." Ibid.

p. 93, "trying to get . . ." Cheney, *Man Out of Time,* 52.

p. 93, "I trust you will . . . " *Master of Lightning,* PBS video.

p. 97-98, "In that event . . . field of electricity," Cheney, *Man Out of Time,* 57-58.

CHAPTER EIGHT: Master of Lightning

p. 103-104, "In a few minutes . . . principle cannot fail," Seifert, *Wizard,* 191.

p. 105, "My submarine boat . . ." Nikola Tesla, "Torpedo Boat Without a Crew," *Current Literature,* February 1899, 136-137.

p. 107, "Mr. Tesla fools himself . . ." Seifert, *Wizard,* 196.

p. 107, "I remember that when . . ." Tesla, *My Inventions,* 203.

p. 109, "My coils are producing . . ." Cheney, *Man Out of Time,* 158.

p. 109-110, "All things arranged . . . " Ibid., 160.

p. 111, "Observations made last night . . ." Seifert, *Wizard,* 219.

p. 114, "Do not worry . . ." Ibid., 223.

CHAPTER NINE: Wardenclyffe
p. 117, "worth 100 times . . ." Ibid., 256.
p. 118, "Marconi is a donkey," Cheney, *Man Out of Time,* 221.
p. 119, "If I would have . . . any further advances," Ibid., 198.
p. 121, "Has anything happened . . ." Ibid., 207.
p. 121, "I'm ever in so much . . ." Seifert, *Wizard,* 324.
p. 123, "other inventions which . . ." Ibid., 338.
p. 124, "something new . . ." Cheney, *Man Out of Time,* 228.

CHAPTER TEN: Setbacks
p. 128, "My airship will have . . ." Frank Parker Stockbridge, "Tesla's New Monarch of Mechanics," *New York Herald Tribune,* October 15, 1911.
p. 129, "I am almost despairing . . ." Cheney, *Man Out of Time,* 231.
p. 133-134, "Were we to seize . . ." Ibid., 262.
p. 136, "Sometimes I feel that . . ." Seifert, *Wizard,* 414.
p. 137-138, "I have been feeding . . ." O'Neill, *Prodigal Genius,* 317.

CHAPTER ELEVEN: The Death Ray
p. 141, "will send concentrated beams . . ." Seifert, *Wizard,* 425.
p. 141, "This new beam of mine . . ." Helen Welsheimer, "Dr. Tesla Visions the End of Aircraft in War," *Everyday Week Magazine,* October 21, 1934.
p. 142, "an entirely new . . . humanity itself," Seifert, *Wizard,* 421.
p. 143, "I think that nothing . . ." Ibid.
p. 144, "How are you . . ." Ibid., 437.
p. 148, "might make certain . . ." Ibid., 448.

BIBLIOGRAPHY

Anderson, Frederick, ed. *Mark Twain's Notebooks and Journals.* Vol. 3, *1883-1891.* Berkeley, CA: University of California Press, 1979.

Berger, Melvin. *Switch On, Switch Off.* New York: Harper and Row, 1989.

Cheney, Margaret. *Tesla: Man Out of Time.* New York: Dell Publishing, 1981.

Hunt, Inez and Wanda Draper. *Lightning in His Hands: The Life Story of Nikola Tesla.* Hawthorne, CA: Omni Publications, 1977.

Martin, T. C. "The Burning of Tesla's Laboratory." *Engineering Magazine,* April 1895.

O'Neill, John J. *Prodigal Genius.* New York: Ives Washburn, 1944.

Petkovich, Dragislav. "A Visit to Nikola Tesla." *Politika*, April 27, 1927.

Seifert, Marc J. *Wizard: The Life and Times of Nikola Tesla, Biography of a Genius.* New York: Citadel Press, 1996.

Smith, William T., ed. *Schaum's Easy Outline: Basic Electricity.* New York: McGraw-Hill, 2002.

Stephenson, W. T. "Electric Light of the Future." *Outlook,* March 9, 1895.

Stockbridge, Frank Parker. "Tesla's New Monarch of Mechanics." *New York Herald Tribune,* October 15, 1911.

Tesla, Nikola. *My Inventions.* Edited by Ben Johnston. Austin, TX: Hart Brothers, 1982.

----------. "Torpedo Boat Without a Crew." *Current Literature,* February 1899.

"Tesla at 75." *Time*, July 20, 1931.

Welsheimer, Helen. "Dr. Tesla Visions the End of Aircraft in War." *Everyday Week Magazine*, October 21, 1934.

WEB SITES

http://www.pbs.org/tesla/
A comprehensive and informative site from PBS.

http://www.uspto.gov/
The official Web site of the United States Patent and Trademark Office.

http://www.teslasociety.com
A site dedicated to keeping Tesla's memory alive.

http://edison.rutgers.edu/
A collection of Edison's papers with information about his life.

http://www.tomedison.org/
The Edison Birthplace Museum's Web site.

INDEX